CLASSIC PRAYERS
FOR
EVERY
NEED

Edited by Donna K. Maltese

BARBOUR BOOKS
An Imprint of Barbour Publishing, Inc.

© 2017 by Barbour Publishing, Inc.

Print ISBN 978-1-68322-016-9

All scripture quotations are taken from the King James Version of the Bible.

Published by Barbour Books, an imprint of Barbour Publishing, Inc., P.O. Box 719, Uhrichsville, Ohio 44683, www.barbourbooks.com

Our mission is to publish and distribute inspirational products offering exceptional value and biblical encouragement to the masses.

Member of the
Evangelical Christian
Publishers Association

Printed in the United States of America.

Contents

INTRODUCTION

What to pray? What to say? Those are the questions that ring in our ears when we cannot seem to find the words we long to bring to God's attention. And although Romans 8:26–27 says, "the Spirit itself maketh intercession for us with groanings which cannot be uttered," it is a tremendous help to have strong and meaningful words to bring to and speak into God's ears and into our own spirits.

E. M. Bounds wrote that "God shapes the world by prayer. Prayers are deathless. They outlive the lives of those who uttered them." I would purpose that prayers, even those centuries old, continue to shape us today, and outlive the lives of those who have written them!

That's why you now have this amazing resource at your fingertips! Here is a collection of over 280 powerful prayers from over 140 Christians who have walked the path you now travel. These prayers, some from ages past, continue to apply to the problems and challenges you have today, helping you to successfully navigate your thoughts away from your troubles and toward the love and power of God.

Classic Prayers for Every Need covers 57 topical sections, each one opening with a devotional thought, followed by five or more prayers, as well as a quote relating to that topic.

No matter what your plea or need, here you will find the words you seek to touch God's heart and reshape your own, morning, noon, and night.

May the prayers within this book bless you and your prayer life. Amen.

Contributors

Alcuin, c. 735–804; English scholar, poet, and teacher.

Andrewes, Lancelot, 1555–1626; English bishop, scholar, and writer.

Arndt, Johann, 1555–1621; German Lutheran author and theologian.

Arnold, Thomas, 1795–1842; English educator and historian.

Appleton, George, 1902–1993; Anglican bishop and writer.

Astley, Jacob, 1579–1652; First Baron Astley of Reading, England, and infantry commander.

Baillie, John, 1886–1960; Scottish minister and author.

Barclay, William, 1907–1978; Scottish author and writer.

Baring-Gould, Sabine, 1834–1924; Anglican priest, novelist, and hymn writer.

Becon, Thomas, c. 1511–1567; English cleric and reformer.

Beecher, Henry Ward, 1813–1887; American preacher, reformer, author, and speaker.

Blake, William, 1757–1827; English artist and poet.

Boehme, Jacob, 1575–1624; German shoemaker, writer, mystic, and theologian.

Bonhoeffer, Dietrich, 1906–1945; German Lutheran pastor, theologian, and writer.

Bounds, E. M. [Edward McKendree], 1835–1913; American attorney, author, and clergyman.

Bright, William, 1824–1901; English historian and Anglican priest.

Brother Lawrence, 1614–1691; French lay brother in a Carmelite monastery and author.

Browning, Robert, 1812–1889; English poet and playwright.

Buechner, Frederick, 1926– ; American writer and minister.

Bunyan, John, 1628–1688; English writer and preacher.

Calvin, John, 1509–1564; French theologian and father of Calvinism.

Carey, William, 1761-1834; British missionary and Baptist minister.

Carpenter, Mary, 1807–1877; English educator, social reformer, and writer.

Cassian, John, 360–435; Christian monk and theologian.

Catherine of Siena, 1347–1380; Dominican nun.

Chambers, Oswald, 1874–1917; Scottish evangelist, teacher, and author.

Channing, William Ellery, 1780–1842; Unitarian preacher in the US.

Chrysostom, John, c. 347–407; Archbishop of Constantinople and saint.

Cosin, John, 1594-1672; English writer.

Dawson, George, 1821–1876; English preacher and speaker.

de Chardin, Teilhard, 1881–1955; French philosopher and Jesuit priest.

de Sales, Francis, 1567–1622; Bishop of Geneva, author, and Roman Catholic saint.

Donne, John, 1572–1631; English poet, lawyer, and priest.

Dostoevsky, Fyodor, 1821–1881; Russian novelist.

Edwards, Jonathan, 1703–1758; American preacher.

Élizabeth of France, 1764–1794; French princess known for her piety.

Erasmus [aka Desiderius Erasmus Roterodamus], 1466–1536; Dutch Catholic priest, teacher, and author.

Eusebius of Caesarea [aka Eusebius Pamphili], 260/265–339/340; Roman historian, writer, and bishop.

Fénelon, Francois, 1651–1715; Roman Catholic bishop, poet, and writer.

Foote, Henry W., 1794–1869; American minister and author.

Fox, George, 1624–1691; English founder of the Quakers.

Fuller, Thomas, 1608–1661; English historian, churchman, and author.

Gordon, Charles George, 1833–1885; British army officer and committed Christian.

Gordon, S. D. [Samuel Dickey], 1859–1936; American speaker and author.

Goudge, Elizabeth, 1900–1984; English author.

Grey, Lady Jane [aka Lady Jane Dudley or the Nine-Day Queen], 1536/1537–1554; English noblewoman and committed Protestant.

Grou, Jean Nicholas, 1731–1803; French Roman Catholic author.

Guyon, Jeanne [aka Jeanne-Marie Bouvier de la Motte-Guyon, Madam Guyon] 1648–1717; French mystic and writer.

Hallesby, Ole, 1879–1961; Norwegian theologian, author, and educator.

Hammarskjöld, Dag, 1905–1961; Swedish diplomat, author, and second Secretary-General of the United Nations.

Hare, Maria, [aka, Twtaria Lycester/Mrs. Augustus Hare] 1798–1870; English writer.

Hatch, Edwin, 1835–1889; English theologian and composer.

Henry, Matthew, 1662–1714, Wales-born minister and author.

Herbert, George, 1593–1633; Welsh poet, speaker, and priest.

Hickes, George, 1642–1715; English rector, chaplain, and writer.

Houselander, Caryll, 1901–1954; English writer, artist, and poet.

Hunter, Leslie, 1890–1983; Bishop of Sheffield and author.

Jarrett, Bede, 1881–1934; English Dominican friar, Catholic priest, and author.

Jenks, Benjamin, 1646–1724; English curate and author.

Johnson, Samuel, 1709–1784; English author, poet, and moralist.

Jowett, John Henry, 1863–1923; British Protestant preacher and author.

Julian of Norwich, 1342–c. 1416; Englishwoman, author, and theologian.

Kempis, Thomas á, 1380–1471; Dutch author of *The Imitation of Christ*.

Kierkegaard, Søren, 1813–1855; Danish poet, philosopher, theologian, and author.

Lewis, C. S. [Clive Staples], 1898–1963; British writer of fiction and nonfiction, teacher, poet, speaker, and theologian.

Livingstone, David, 1813–1873; Scottish doctor, missionary, and explorer of Africa.

Luther, Martin, 1483–1546; German professor, composer, monk, and leader of the Protestant Reformation.

King Jr., Martin Luther, 1929–1968; American preacher, activist, humanitarian, and leader of the African-American Civil Rights Movement in the US.

MacDonald, George, 1824–1905; Scottish author, poet, and minister.

Mansfield, Katherine, 1888–1923; New Zealand short story writer.

Marshall, Catherine, 1914–1983; American writer and wife of minister Peter Marshall.

Marshall, Peter, 1902–1949; Scottish American preacher, pastor, and Chaplain of US Senate.

Martineau, James, 1805–1900; Unitarian minister, philosopher, theologian, and writer.

Matheson, George, 1842–1906; Scottish clergyman, writer, and hymn writer.

McComb, Samuel, 1864–1938; Irish-born, Oxford-educated Canadian professor, and American minister, writer, and speaker.

Mechthild of Magdeburg, c. 1207–1282/1294; German mystic and poet.

Merton, Thomas, 1915–1968; American monk and writer.

Meyer, F. B. [Frederick Brotherton], 1847–1929; Baptist preacher and writer.

Miller, J. R. [James Russel], 1840–1912; American author and pastor.

Milner-White, Eric, 1884–1963; Priest, soldier, and Dean of York in the Church of England.

Moody, D. L. [aka Dwight L. Moody], 1837–1899; American evangelist, publisher, and author.

More, Sir Thomas, 1478–1535; English author, statesman, and lawyer.

Mother Teresa [born Agnes Gonxha Bojaxhiu], 1910–1997; Roman Catholic nun and missionary.

Muggeridge, Malcolm, 1903–1990; British author and agnostic who became Christian.

Murray, Andrew, 1828–1917; South-African-born Scotsman, author and pastor.

Naylor, James, 1616–1660; English Quaker leader, evangelist, minister, and writer.

Newman, John Henry, 1801–1890; English Roman-Catholic Cardinal.

Niebuhr, Reinhold, 1892–1971; American minister, theologian, ethicist, seminary professor, and writer.

Newton, John, 1725–1807; British slaver trader who became an abolitionist and Christian.

Oldham, John, 1653–1683; English poet and educator.

Oosterhuis, Huub, 1933– ; Dutch theologian and poet.

Orchard, William Edwin, 1877–1955; minister, priest, writer, and pacifist.

Origen, c. 184–254; early Christian theologian.

Oxenden, Ashton, 1808–1892; English clergyman, author, and Bishop of Montreal.

Patrick, Simon, 1626–1707; English theologian, bishop, and writer.

Penn, William, 1644–1718; English Quaker, philosopher, and founder of Pennsylvania.

Pope, Alexander, 1688–1744; English poet.

Pusey, Edward B., 1800–1882; English churchman, professor, and author.

Quoist, Michel, 1918–1997; French catholic priest and writer.

Rahner, Karl, 1904–1984; German Jesuit priest and writer.

Rauschenbusch, Walter, 1861–1918; American theologian and pastor.

Rice, Helen Steiner, 1900–1981; American writer and poet.

Roberts, Evan, 1878–1951; Welsh revivalist, poet, and speaker.

Rossetti, Christina, 1830–1894; English poet.

Sailer, Michael [aka Johann Michael Sailer], 1751–1832; German professor and bishop.

Saint Anatolius, 449–458; Greek Patriarch of Constantinople.

Saint Anselm, 1033–1109; monk, abbot, and philosopher.

Saint Augustine [aka Augustine of Hippo], 354–430]; theologian, philosopher, and writer.

Saint Basil the Great, c. 329–379; Greek bishop, theologian, and writer.

Saint Bede the Venerable, 672/673–735; English monk, scholar, and author.

Saint Benedict of Nursia, c. 480–543 or 547; saint.

Saint Bernard [aka Bernard of Clairvaux], 1091–1153; French abbot, author, and "Doctor of the Church."

Saint Clement of Rome, died 99; Bishop of Rome from 88 to 99.

Saint Columba of Iona, 521–597; Irish abbot and missionary.

Saint Columbanus, 543–615; Irish-born founder of monasteries, preacher, and poet.

Saint Francis of Assisi [born Giovanni di Pietro di Bernardone], 1181/1182–1226; Italian Roman Catholic friar, preacher, writer, and poet.

Saint Gregory of Nazianzus, c. 329–390; Archbishop of Constantinople, theologian, and philosopher.

Saint Ignatius of Loyola, 1491–1556; Spanish knight, hermit, and priest.

Saint Patrick, 5th Century; Romano-British Christian missionary, bishop, and saint of Ireland.

Saint Peter Claver, 1581–1654; Spanish priest and missionary.

Saint Richard of Chichester [aka Richard de Wych], 1197–1253; bishop.

Saint Teresa of Avila, 1515–1582; Spanish nun and author.

Saint Thérèse of Lisieux [aka Marie Françoise Thérèse Martin], 1873–1897; French nun.

Saint Thomas Aquinas, [aka Tommaso d'Aquino], 1225–1274; Italian friar, Roman Catholic priest, philosopher, and writer.

Sanford, Agnes, c. 1898–1982; American author.

Shakespeare, William, 1564–1616; English poet, actor, and playwright.

Sherman, Frank Dempster, 1860–1916; American poet and professor.

Simpson, A. B. [Albert Benjamin], 1843–1919; Canadian preacher and author.

Slessor, Mary, 1848-1915; Scottish missionary.

Smith, Hannah Whitall, 1832–1911; American Quaker, speaker, and author.

Snowden, Rita, 1907–1999; New Zealand missionary and author.

Spurgeon, Charles, 1834–1892; British preacher and writer.

Starck, Johann Friedrich, 1680–1756; Prussian pastor and hymn writer.

Stevenson, Robert Louis, 1850–1894; Scottish novelist, poet, and essayist.

Taylor, Jeremy, 1613–1667; cleric and author.

Temple, William, 1881–1944; English Bishop, Archbishop, teacher, preacher, and writer.

ten Boom, Corrie, 1892–1983; Dutch Christian and author.

Tersteegen, Gerhard, 1697–1769; German reformed religious writer, speaker, poet, and hymn writer.

Torrey, R. A. [Ruben Archer], 1856–1928; American pastor and writer.

Tozer, A. W. [Aiden Wilson], 1897–1963; American preacher, author, and editor.

Underhill, Evelyn, 1875–1941; English writer and pacifist.

van Beethoven, Ludwig, 1770-1827; German composer and pianist.

van Dyke, Henry, 1852–1933; American clergyman, educator, and author.

Washington, George, 1732-1799; first president of the United States.

Wells, H. G. [Herbert George], 1866–1946; writer of novels, history, and textbooks.

Wesley, Charles, 1707–1788; English preacher and hymn writer.

Wesley, John, 1703–1791; English preacher and writer.

Westcott, Brooke Foss, 1825–1901; British bishop, scholar, and writer.

Wilberforce, William, 1759–1833; English politician and abolitionist.

Williams, Rowland, 1817–1870; British priest, vicar, and professor.

Wilson, Thomas, 1663–1755; English Anglican bishop.

Woolman, John, 1720–1772; North American merchant, essayist, journalist, and Quaker preacher.

ADVERSITY

Jesus said we would have trouble in this life. But we can take courage and joy in the fact that He has overcome the world! In the meantime, we have a God to go to, as did the Psalmist David who trusted God, made Him his refuge "until these calamities be overpast" (Psalm 57:1). So pray and sit tight. God's got you. Whatever adversity you face shall pass.

Let God's promises shine on your problems.
CORRIE TEN BOOM

Lord, open my eyes that I may see, not the visible enemy, but Thy unseen chariots of deliverance.
HANNAH WHITALL SMITH

I do not know, O God, what will happen to me today, I only know that nothing will happen to me but what has been foreseen by You from all eternity, and that is sufficient, O my God, to keep me in peace. I adore Your eternal designs. I submit to them with all my heart. I desire them all and accept them all. I make a sacrifice of everything. I unite this sacrifice to that of Your dear Son, my Savior, begging You by His infinite merits, for the patience in troubles, and the perfect submission which is due to You in all that You will and design for me.

ÉLIZABETH OF FRANCE

O Merciful God, be Thou now unto me a strong tower of defense, I humbly entreat Thee. Give me grace to await Thy leisure, and patiently to bear what Thou doest unto me; nothing doubting or mistrusting Thy goodness toward me; for Thou knowest what is good for me better than I do. Therefore do with me in all things what Thou wilt; only arm me, I beseech Thee, with Thine armor, that I may stand fast; above all things, taking to me the shield of faith; praying always that I may refer myself wholly to Thy will, abiding Thy pleasure, and comforting myself in those troubles which it shall please Thee to send me, seeing such troubles as are profitable for me; and I am assuredly persuaded that all Thou doest cannot but be well; and unto Thee be all honor and glory. Amen.

LADY JANE GREY

O Lord, come quickly and reign on Thy throne,
for now oftentimes something rises up within me,
and tries to take possession of Thy throne: pride,
covetousness, uncleanness, and sloth want to be my
kings; and then evil-speaking, anger, hatred, and the
whole train of vices join with me in warring against
myself, and try to reign over me. I resist them,
I cry out against them, and say, "I have no other
king than Christ." O King of Peace, come and reign
in me, for I will have no king but Thee! Amen.
SAINT BERNARD

Some things have not gone well today. We have had
our troubles. Our hearts have been hurt. You are the
healer—will You heal us? Take the tangled threads
out of our clumsy hands, disentangle them and weave
them into a web of beauty! Take the dark things of
the day's providences, the things that seem wrong,
and by the power of Your grace, transmute them into
blessing. Help us indeed to keep our hands off the
strange, complex affairs of our lives—for we would
only spoil the pattern which You are fashioning in us,
if we attempted to adjust these complicated affairs.
May You take entire charge of the myriad things of
our lives that are beyond our managing, and bring
good and only good out of them.
J. R. MILLER

AFFLICTION

In the midst of affliction, you draw even closer to God. To His love, His sweetness, His abiding presence. Your walk becomes deeper, more meaningful. All you need to do is remember His sacrificial love and allow Him to carry you through (see Isaiah 63:9).

In times of affliction we commonly meet
with the sweetest experiences
of the love of God.
JOHN BUNYAN

Trusting in Your goodness
and great mercy, Lord, I come;
sick—I come to my Savior;
hungry and thirsty—to the well of Life;
needy—to the King of Heaven.
THOMAS Á KEMPIS

Lord, teach me the art of patience whilst I am well, and give me the use of it when I am sick. In that day either lighten my burden or strengthen my back. Make me, who so often in my health have discovered my weakness presuming on my own strength, to be strong in my sickness when I solely rely on Thy assistance.

Thomas Fuller

Lord Jesus be with my spirit, and dwell in my heart by faith. . . . Be with me, O my Savior, everywhere, and at all times. . . .in all events and circumstances of my life: to sanctify and sweeten to me whatever befalls me. And never leave nor forsake me in my present pilgrimage here, till Thou hast brought me safe through all trials and dangers, to be ever with the Lord, there to live in Thy sight and love and glory, world without end. Amen.

Benjamin Jenks

Preserve my soul, O Lord, because it belongs to Thee, and preserve my body because it belongs to my soul. Thou alone dost steer my boat through all its voyage, but hast a more especial care of it, when it comes to a narrow current, or to a dangerous fall of waters. Thou hast a care of the preservation of my body in all the ways of my life; but, in the straits of death, open Thine eyes wider, and enlarge Thy Providence toward me so far that no illness or agony may shake and benumb the soul. Do Thou so make my bed in all my sickness that, being used to Thy hand, I may content with any bed of Thy making. Amen.

JOHN DONNE

Father, lover of life, we pray for those suffering from disease for which, at present, there is no known cure; give them confidence in Your love and never-failing support and a stronger faith in the resurrection. Grant wisdom and perseverance to all working to discover the causes of the disease, so that they see in their labors the ministry of Your Son, who Himself showed forth His divine power by healing those who came to Him.

GEORGE APPLETON

AGING

The great thing about being more mature is the experience you can bring to every situation. And, if you are planted in God, you, like a cedar in Lebabnon, will continue to "bring forth fruit in old age" and "be fat and flourishing" (Psalm 92:14)! So simply stick close to God, and enjoy every moment of your life!

Autumn is really the best of the seasons; and I'm not sure that old age isn't the best part of life.
C. S. Lewis

In thee, O Lord, do I put my trust: let me never be put to confusion. . . . . Be thou my strong habitation, whereunto I may continually resort: thou hast given commandment to save me; for thou art my rock and my fortress. . . . For thou art my hope, O Lord God: thou art my trust from my youth. . . . Cast me not off in the time of old age; forsake me not when my strength faileth. . . . Now also when I am old and greyheaded, O God, forsake me not; until I have shewed thy strength unto this generation, and thy power to every one that is to come.
Psalm 71:1, 3, 5, 9, 18

Almighty God, by whose mercy my life has
continued for another year, I pray that, as my years
increase, my sins may not increase. As age advances,
let me become more open, more faithful and
more trusting in You. Let me not be distracted
by lesser things from what is truly important.
And if I become infirm as I grow old, may I
not be overwhelmed by self-pity or bitterness.
Continue and increase Your loving kindness
toward me so that, when You finally call me
to Yourself, I may enter into eternal happiness
with You, through Christ my Lord.

Samuel Johnson

May Christ-Omega keep me always young "to the
greater glory of God." For old age comes from Him,
old age leads on to Him, and old age will touch me
only in so far as He wills. To be "young" means to be
hopeful, energetic, smiling—and clear-sighted. May
I accept death in whatever guise it may come to me
in Christ-Omega, that is within the process of the
development of life. A smile (inward and outward)
means facing with sweetness and gentleness whatever
befalls me. Jesus-Omega, grant me to serve You,
to proclaim You, to glorify You, to make You
manifest, to the very end through all the time
that remains to me of life, and above all through
my death. Desperately, Lord Jesus, I commit to
Your care my last active years, and my death;
do not let them impair or spoil my work I
have so dreamed of achieving for You.

Teilhard de Chardin

O Lord, our God, under the shadow of Thy wings
let us hope. Thou wilt support us, both when
little, and even to gray hairs. When our strength
is of Thee, it is strength; but, when our own, it is
feebleness. We return unto Thee, O Lord, that from
their weariness our souls may rise toward Thee,
leaning on the things which Thou hast created,
and passing on to Thyself, Who hast wonderfully
made them; for with Thee is refreshment
and true strength. Amen.

SAINT AUGUSTINE

Father in heaven, draw our hearts to You, that our
hearts may be where our treasures ought to be, that
our minds and thoughts may look to Your kingdom,
whose citizens we are. Thus, when You shall call
us hence, our departure may not be a painful
separation from this world, but a joyous meeting
with You. Perhaps a long road still lies before us.
Yet sometimes our strength is taken from us,
a faintness overcomes us, like a mist before our
eyes, so that we are in darkness of the night; restless
desires stir within us, impatient, wild longings, and
the heart groans in anxious anticipation of what
is to come: O Lord our God, do teach us then,
and strengthen in our hearts the conviction
that in life as in death we belong to You.

SØREN KIERKEGAARD

BLESSINGS

God has a storehouse of blessings just waiting for you. All you need to do is ask in His name and will. For God has said He will "open you the windows of heaven, and pour you out a blessing, that there shall not be room enough to receive it" (Malachi 3:10). Your job? To be a blessing to others. Now go, ask, and watch God work.

> However many blessings we expect from God,
> His infinite liberality will always exceed
> all our wishes and our thoughts.
> JOHN CALVIN

And Jabez called on the God of Israel, saying, Oh that thou wouldest bless me indeed, and enlarge my coast, and that thine hand might be with me, and that thou wouldest keep me from evil, that it may not grieve me! And God granted him that which he requested.
1 CHRONICLES 4:10

O Lord, my God, teach me to pray for the right
blessings. Steer the vessel of my life toward Yourself,
the peaceful harbor for storm-tossed souls. Show
me the course I should sail, renew a willing spirit
within me. May Your Spirit curb my wandering
senses and help me to observe Your laws.
Gladden my heart with Your glorious presence
within. For Yours is the glory and the
praise of all the saints forever.

SAINT BASIL THE GREAT

We come to Thee with our weakness, asking Thee
for strength. Help us always to be of good cheer.
Let us not be disheartened by difficulties. Let
us never doubt Thy love or any of Thy promises.
Give us grace to be encouragers of others, never
discouragers. Let us not go about with sadness or
fear among men, but may we be a benediction to
everyone we meet, always making life easier,
never harder, for those who come within our
influence. Help us to be as Christ to others,
that they may see something of His love in our
lives and learn to love Him in us. We beseech
Thee to hear us, to receive our prayer, and to
forgive our sins, for Jesus Christ's sake. Amen.

J. R. MILLER

May my whole being, O God, be one thanksgiving unto Thee; may all within me praise Thee and love Thee; for all which Thou hast forgiven, and for all which Thou hast given; for Thine unknown hidden blessings, and for those which, in my negligence or thoughtlessness, I passed over; for any and every gift of nature or of grace; for my power of loving; for all blessings within and without; and for all which Thou hast yet in store for me; for everything whereby Thou hast drawn me to Thyself, whether joy or sorrow; for all whereby Thou willest to make Thine own forever. Amen.

EDWARD B. PUSEY

CHARACTER

Each day people take pains to make sure they look good on the outside. But God knows beauty is only skin deep. What lies in your heart is the true teller of who you are. Spend some moments today shaping up your character by seeking to follow Jesus' example. It'll change your inner—and outer—life.

Conduct is what we do, character is what we are.
E. M. BOUNDS

We must praise Your goodness that You have left nothing undone to draw us to Yourself. But one thing we ask of You, our God, not to cease to work in our improvement. Let us tend toward You, no matter by what means, and be fruitful in good works, for the sake of Jesus Christ our Lord.
LUDWIG VAN BEETHOVEN

O God, our Father, help us all through this day so to live that we may bring help to others, credit to ourselves and to the name we bear, and joy to those that love us, and to You. Cheerful when things go wrong; persevering when things are difficult; serene when things are irritating. Enable us to be: helpful to those in difficulties; kind to those in need; sympathetic to those whose hearts are sore and sad. Grant that: nothing may make us lose our tempers; nothing may take away our joy; nothing may ruffle our peace; nothing may make us bitter toward anyone. So grant that through all this day all with whom we work, and all those whom we meet, may see in us the reflection of the master, whose we are, and whom we seek to serve. This we ask for Your love's sake.

WILLIAM BARCLAY

O God, stay with me; let no word cross my lips that is not Your word, no thoughts enter my mind that are not Your thoughts, no deed ever be done or entertained by me that is not Your deed.

MALCOLM MUGGERIDGE

O Thou, Whose name is Love Who never turnest away from the cry of Thy needy children, give ear to my prayer this morning. Make this a day of blessings to me, and make me a blessing to others. Keep all evil away from me. Preserve me from outward transgression and from secret sin. Help me to control my temper. May I check the first risings of anger or sullenness. If I meet with unkindness or ill-treatment, give me that charity which suffereth long and beareth all things. Make me kind and gentle toward all, loving even those who love me not. Let me live this day as if it were to be my last. O my God, show me the path that Thou wouldest have me to follow. May I take no step that is not ordered by Thee, and go nowhere except Thou, Lord, go with me. Amen.

ASHTON OXENDEN

By virtue of Thy victory, give us also, I entreat Thee, victory. Let Thy pierced heart win us to love Thee, Thy torn hands incite us to every good work, Thy wounded feet urge us on errands of mercy, Thy crown of thorns prick us out of sloth, Thy thirst draw us to thirst after the Living Water Thou givest; let Thy life be our pattern while we live and Thy death our triumph over death when we come to die.

CHRISTINA ROSSETTI

CHILDREN

Children young and old, ours or others', are constantly looking to us as an example. And as we teach them what it means to be a follower of Christ, so they teach us about where we may be falling short. So, tread carefully, teach endlessly, and learn constantly, with and from them. Most of all, love, forgive, and enjoy them, as your Father always loves, forgives, and enjoys you.

The soul is healed by being with children.
FYODOR DOSTOEVSKY

Give, I pray Thee, to all children grace reverently
to love their parents, and lovingly to obey them.
Teach us all that filial duty never ends or lessens;
and bless all parents in their children,
and all children in their parents.
CHRISTINA ROSSETTI

Heavenly Father, from whom all fatherhood in
heaven and earth is named, bless, we beg You,
all children, and give to their parents and to all
in whose charge they may be, Your Spirit of wisdom
and love; so that the home in which they grow
up may be to them an image of Your kingdom,
and the care of their parents a likeness of Your
love; through Jesus Christ our Lord.
LESLIE HUNTER

Bless my children with healthful bodies, with good
understandings, with the graces and gifts of Your
Spirit, with sweet dispositions and holy habits,
and sanctify them throughout in their bodies and
souls and spirits, and keep them unblamable
to the coming of the Lord Jesus.
JEREMY TAYLOR

Grant to us, O Father, the wisdom that is necessary
in all the conduct of life. And grant that even
our mistakes may rise up to guide us and when
we behold the mistakes of others, while we seek
to rescue them and to sympathize with them,
grant that we may read likewise the
lessons which they make for us.

HENRY WARD BEECHER

Almighty God and heavenly Father, we thank You
for the children which You have given us; give us
also grace to train them in Your faith, fear, and
love; that as they advance in years they may
grow in grace, and may hereafter be found in
the number of Your children; through
Jesus Christ our Lord. Amen.

JOHN COSIN

CHRISTLIKENESS

When you accept Christ, you are on your way to becoming like Him—not just in your heart, but in your mind, thoughts, actions, and attitude toward others. It is when you put aside your ego and negative thinking, your selfishness and love of the world, that He finds room to shine through.

The beauty of believers consists in their resemblance to Jesus Christ.
MATTHEW HENRY

Dear Jesus, help me to spread Thy fragrance everywhere I go. Flood my soul with Thy spirit and love. Penetrate and possess my whole being so utterly that all my life may only be a radiance of Thine. Shine through me and be so in me that every soul I come in contact with may feel Thy presence in my soul. Let them look up and see no longer me but only Jesus. Stay with me and then I shall begin to shine as You shine, so to shine as to be a light to others.
MOTHER TERESA
from the video *Everyone, Everywhere*

Let us praise Him then, for His life in our spirits, increasing in us the consciousness of being His children, light of His light, life of His life. And let us rejoice in His life in our minds, directing and arranging our thoughts, increasing our mental powers, giving us a better grasp of business and more wisdom in every line of work we undertake. Let us thank Him for His life in our hearts, ordering and controlling our emotions and filling us with His own love. And let us give thanks for His life in our bodies, recreating them after the image of His perfect health and strength.

AGNES SANFORD

O Lord Jesus Christ. . .save us from the error of
wishing to admire You instead of being willing to
follow You and to resemble You.
SØREN KIERKEGAARD

Help me, O Lord, to descend into the depths of
my being, below my conscious and subconscious life
until I discover my real self, that which is given me
from Thee, the divine likeness in which I am made
and into which I am to grow, the place
where Your Spirit communes with mine,
the spring from which all my life rises.
GEORGE APPLETON

Lord, make me according to Thy heart.
BROTHER LAWRENCE

CONTENTMENT

No matter what the world says you need, you know the truth: God is all you need. He alone suffices. In Him, you will never lack any good thing. That is true contentment—in this world and the next.

Let nothing disturb you; let nothing dismay you; all things pass: God never changes. Patience attains all it strives for. He who has God finds he lacks nothing; God alone suffices.
SAINT TERESA OF AVILA

Almighty God, who knowest our necessities before we ask, and our ignorance in asking: Set free Thy servants from all anxious thoughts for the morrow; give us contentment with Thy good gifts; and confirm our faith that according as we seek Thy kingdom, Thou wilt not suffer us to lack any good thing; through Jesus Christ our Lord.
SAINT AUGUSTINE

Grant, gracious Father, that I may never dispute the
reasonableness of Thy will, but ever close with it,
as the best that can happen. Prepare me always for
what Thy providence shall bring forth. Let me never
murmur, be dejected, or impatient, under any of the
troubles of this life, but ever find rest and comfort
in this, this is the will of my Father, and of my
God; grant this for Jesus Christ's sake. Amen.
THOMAS WILSON

God, of Your goodness, give me Yourself; for You
are sufficient for me. I cannot properly ask anything
less, to be worthy of You. If I were to ask less, I
should always be in want. In You alone do I have all.
JULIAN OF NORWICH

O Lord God, grant us always, whatever the
world may say, to content ourselves with what
Thou wilt say, and to care only for Thine
approval, which will outweigh all words.
CHARLES GEORGE GORDON

Take, Lord, all my liberty. Receive my memory,
my understanding, and my whole will.
Whatever I have and possess, You have given to
me; to You I restore it wholly, and to Your will
I utterly surrender it for Your direction. Give me
the love of You only, with Your grace, and I am
rich enough; nor ask I anything beside.
SAINT IGNATIUS OF LOYOLA

COURAGE

With God on your side, you have all the courage you need. The same courage that powered up Joseph, Moses, Deborah, Jael, Gideon, David, Abigail, Jehoshaphat, Esther, and Mary is available to you today. No matter what lies near or before you, glean courage from the fact that God stands with and behind you.

We must constantly build dykes of courage
to hold back the flood of fear.
MARTIN LUTHER KING JR.

The Lord is my helper, I will not fear—I will not
be haunted by apprehension. . . . The Lord is my
Helper, this second, in my present outlook. . . . I will
not fear. It does not matter what evil or wrong may
be in the way. . . . The Lord is my helper.
OSWALD CHAMBERS
My Utmost for His Highest, June 5 reading

Lord, purge our eyes to see
Within the seed a tree,
Within the glowing egg a bird,
Within the shroud a butterfly.
Till, taught by such we see
Beyond all creatures, Thee
And hearken to Thy tender word
And hear its "Fear not; it is I."
CHRISTINA ROSSETTI

May He give us all the courage that we need to go
the way He shepherds us, that when He calls we
may go unfrightened. If He bids us come to Him
across the waters, that unfrightened we may go.
And if He bids us climb the hill, may we not notice
that it is a hill, mindful only of the happiness of His
company. He made us for Himself, that we should
travel with Him and see Him at His last in
His unveiled beauty in the abiding city, where
He is light and happiness and endless home.
BEDE JARRETT

O Thou who art heroic love, keep alive in our hearts
that adventurous spirit which makes men scorn the
way of safety, so that Thy will be done. For so only,
O Lord, shall we be worthy of those courageous
souls who in every age have ventured
all in obedience to Thy call, and for whom the
trumpets have sounded on the other side;
through Jesus Christ our Lord.
JOHN OLDHAM

Make us, O blessed Master, strong in heart,
full of courage, fearless of danger, holding pain
and danger cheap when they lie in the path of duty.
May we be strengthened with all might
by Thy Spirit in our hearts.
F. B. MEYER

DEATH

Nothing can separate you from the God who holds in His embrace both the living and the dead. So no matter where you are, in heaven or on earth, you are in the realm of love where He and all that have gone before reside. Death—it's not an ending. It's a new level of being with the Lord of Love.

> I do not wait for the undertaker,
> but for the Uptaker.
> CORRIE TEN BOOM

> Jesus, Lover of my soul,
> Let me to Thy bosom fly,
> While the nearer waters roll,
> While the tempest still is high:
> Hide me, O my Savior, hide,
> Till the storm of life is past;
> Safe into the haven guide,
> O receive my soul at last.
> CHARLES WESLEY

O Father, support me all the day long of this troublous life, until the shadows lengthen, and the evening comes, and the busy world is hushed, and the fever of life is over, and my work is done. Then, dear Father, in Thy mercy grant me a safe lodging, a holy rest, and a peace at the last; through Jesus Christ, Thy Son and my Lord. Amen.

JOHN HENRY NEWMAN

Bring us, O Lord God, at our last awakening into the house and gate of heaven to enter into that gate and dwell in that house, where there shall be no darkness nor dazzling, but one equal light; no noise nor silence, but one equal music; no fears nor hopes, but one equal possession; no ends nor beginnings, but one equal eternity; in the habitations of Thy glory and dominion, world without end.

JOHN DONNE

O Lord our God, from whom neither life nor
death can separate those who trust in Thy love,
and whose love holds in its embrace Thy children
in this world and in the next: So unite us to Thyself
that in fellowship with Thee we may always be
united to our loved ones whether here or there:
give us courage, constancy and hope; through Him
who died and was buried and rose again
for us, Jesus Christ our Lord.

WILLIAM TEMPLE

We give back to You, O God, those whom You gave
to us. You did not lose them when You gave them
to us, and we do not lose them by their return to
You. Your dear Son has taught us that life is eternal
and love cannot die. So death is only a horizon, and
a horizon is only the limit of our sight. Open our
eyes to see more clearly, and draw us closer to You
that we may know that we are nearer to our loved
ones, who are with You. You have told us that You
are preparing a place for us: prepare for us also that
happy place, that where You are we may also be
always, O dear Lord of life and death.

WILLIAM PENN

DEPRESSION

No matter how far down you may go with the troubles of this world, there is One who reaches out, who has the power to lift you out of the muck and mire, the dread and the dark. His name is the Lord of Light and Life. Reach out your hand, connect with your Savior, and find the peace and joy awaiting you in Him.

When a train goes through a tunnel and it gets dark, you don't throw away the ticket and jump off. You sit still and trust the engineer.

CORRIE TEN BOOM

Lord, hold me up! Hold me,
Lord, by my right hand!
CHARLES SPURGEON

O Lord, my God! The amazing horrors of darkness
were gathered about me, and covered me all over,
and I saw no way to go forth; I felt the depth and
extent of the misery of my fellow-creatures separate
from the Divine harmony, and it was heavier than I
could bear, and I was crushed down under it; lifted
up my hand, I stretched out my arm but there was
none to help me; I looked round about, and was
amazed. In the depths of misery, O Lord,
I remembered that Thou art omnipotent;
that I had called Thee Father; and I felt that
I loved Thee, and I was made quiet in my will,
and I waited for deliverance from Thee.

JOHN WOOLMAN

O Lord God, my soul is sorrowful, sometimes,
even unto tears; sometimes also my spirit is
disquieted, by reason of impending sufferings.
I long after the joy of Thy peace, the peace of Thy
children I earnestly crave. If Thou give peace,
if Thou pour into me holy joy, the soul of Thy
servant shall be full of melody, and shall
become devout in Thy praise. Amen.
THOMAS Á KEMPIS

And now unto Him who is able to keep us from
falling and lift us from the dark valley of despair
to the mountains of hope, from the midnight of
desperation to the daybreak of joy; to Him be
power and authority for ever and ever. Amen.
MARTIN LUTHER KING JR.

O God, animate us to cheerfulness. May we have a joyful sense of our blessings, learn to look on the bright circumstances of our lot, and maintain a perpetual contentedness under Thy allotments. Fortify our minds against disappointment and calamity. Preserve us from despondency, from yielding to dejection. Teach us that no evil is intolerable but a guilty conscience, and that nothing can hurt us, if, with true loyalty of affection, we keep Thy commandments and take refuge in Thee; through Jesus Christ our Lord. Amen.

WILLIAM ELLERY CHANNING

DIRECTION

Each day you choose which path you are going to follow. If you choose your own, you may find yourself drifting off course in turbulent waters. But if you align your will with God's and listen for His voice saying, "This is the way" (Isaiah 30:21), you know you'll be cruising in the right direction, with God at the helm.

It is our part to allow as small a space as possible to intervene between His footsteps and our own.
F. B. MEYER

Lord, we've tried everything we can think of. Every road has seemed a dead end. Doors have been so consistently shut in our faces that You must be trying to teach us something. Tell us what it is—
CATHERINE MARSHALL
Beyond Ourselves, p. 91

My God, I want Thy guidance and direction in all I do. Let Thy wisdom counsel me, Thy hand lead me, and Thine arm support me. I put myself into Thy hands. Breathe into my soul holy and heavenly desires. Conform me to Thine own image. Make me like my Savior. Enable me in some measure to live here on earth as He lived, and to act in all things as He would have acted.

ASHTON OXENDEN

O God our Father, hear me, who am trembling in this darkness, and stretch forth Thy hand unto me; hold forth Thy light before me; recall me from my wanderings; and, Thou being my guide, may I be restored to myself and to Thee.

SAINT AUGUSTINE

Heavenly Father, here I am. I am Thy property. Thou hast bought me with a price. I acknowledge Thine ownership, and surrender myself and all that I am absolutely to Thee. Send me where Thou wilt; do with me what Thou wilt; use me as Thou wilt.
R. A. TORREY

Lord, help me! Lord, help me! Teach me what to ask for! Teach me how to ask for it! Teach me what to think of next! Teach me what to do next.
CHARLES SPURGEON

Discouragement

Some days you may feel as if you cannot go on. But God is always ready to reenergize you, giving you the hope, power, and courage to continue. He has set His promised land before you. Now "go up and possess it, as the LORD God of thy fathers hath said unto thee; fear not, neither be discouraged" (DEUTERONOMY 1:21).

Should we feel at times disheartened and discouraged, a simple movement of heart toward God will renew our powers. Whatever he may demand of us, he will give us at the moment the strength and courage that we need.
FRANCOIS FÉNELON

Maker of me, go on making me, and let me help Thee. Come, oh Father, here I am: let us go on. I know my words are those of a child, but it is Thy child that prays to Thee. It is Thy dark I walk in, it is Thy hand I hold.
GEORGE MACDONALD

O Lord, our God, we desire to feel Thee near us
in spirit and in body at this time. We know that
in Thee we live and move and have our being, but
we are cast down and easily disquieted, and we
wander in many a sad wilderness where we lose
the conscious experience of Thy presence. Yet the
deepest yearning of our hearts is unto Thee. As the
heart panteth after the waterbrooks, so pant our
souls after Thee, O God. Nothing less than Thyself
can still the hunger or quench the thirst with
which Thou hast inspired us. Power of our souls!
enter Thou into them and fit them for Thyself,
making them pure with Christ's purity,
loving and lovable with His love.
SAMUEL MCCOMB

Here, Lord, I abandon myself to Thee. I have tried
in every way I could think of to manage myself,
and to make myself what I know I ought to be but
have always failed. Now I give it up to Thee. Do
Thou take entire possession of me. Work in me all
the good pleasure of Thy will. Mold and fashion me
into such a vessel as seemeth good to Thee.
I leave myself in Thy hands, and I believe Thou
wilt, according to Thy promise, make me into
a vessel unto Thy own honor, "sanctified,
and meet for the Master's use, and
prepared unto every good work."
HANNAH WHITALL SMITH

O God, my God, I am all weakness, but Thou art my Strength; I am ever anew bowed down by any trial, but Thou canst and willest to lift me up. Let me not fail, O God, my Strength; let me not be discouraged, O God, my Hope. Draw me each day, if it be but a little nearer to Thee; make me, each day, if it be but a little less unlike Thee; let me do or bear each day something for love of Thee, whereby I may be fitter for Thee. Let no day pass without my having done something pleasing unto Thee. Thus alone would I live, that I may live more unto Thee; thus would I die, longing to love Thee more. Amen.

EDWARD B. PUSEY

O Lord Jesus Christ, who when on earth wast ever about Thy Father's business: Grant that we may not grow weary in well-doing. Give us grace to do all in Thy name. Be Thou the beginning and the end of all: the pattern whom we follow, the redeemer in whom we trust, the master whom we serve, the friend to whom we look for sympathy. May we never shrink from our duty from any fear of man. Make us faithful unto death; and bring us at last into Thy eternal presence, where with the Father and the Holy Ghost thou livest and reignest for ever.

EDWARD B. PUSEY

DUTIES

Each person has a daily duty to perform. Be it ever so menial or ever so grand, in God's eyes, your work is of equal merit to anyone else's. Your job is to simply keep your faith in the Lord who has called you and perform your tasks to His honor.

The right, practical divinity is this: Believe in Christ, and do thy duty in that state of life to which God has called thee.

MARTIN LUTHER

O Lord, Thou knowest how busy
I must be this day.
If I forget Thee,
do not forget me.

JACOB ASTLEY

O God, who has commanded that no man should be idle, but that we should all work with our hands the thing that is good; grant that I may diligently do my duty in that station of life to which Thou hast been pleased to call me. Give me grace, that I may honestly improve the talents Thou hast committed to my trust, and that no worldly pleasures may ever divert me from the thoughts of the life to come, through Jesus Christ our Lord.

Sabine Baring-Gould

O Lord, I have a busy world around me; eye, ear, and thought will be needed for all my work to be done in that busy world. Now, before I enter upon it, I would commit eye, ear, and thought, to Thee! Do Thou bless them and keep their work Thine, such as, through Thy natural laws, my heart beats and my blood flows without any thought of mine for them, so may my spiritual life hold on its course at those times when my mind cannot consciously turn to Thee to commit each particular thought to Thy service. Hear my prayer for my dear Redeemer's sake. Amen.

Thomas Arnold

Eternal and infinite One, our hours of faithful
duty follow us from the past and do not perish.
Stir within us that we may redeem the time. Great
Giver of the task, we live day and night beneath
Your constant eyes. May we be steadfast through
all faintness of soul and not rest by the roadside
while Your errand waits. Daily may we drive out our
selfishness and delight to bear one another's burden
and uphold each other's faith and hope and love.
May our minds be wholly turned to finish, without
undue disquiet or contention, the work we strive to
do for You. O Watcher of our days and nights,
we would commit them all to You.
JAMES MARTINEAU

The day returns and brings us the petty round
of irritating concerns and duties. Help us to play
the man, help us to perform them with laughter
and kind faces, let cheerfulness abound with
industry. Give us to go blithely on our business
all this day, bring us to our resting beds weary
and content and undishonoured, and grant
us in the end the gift of sleep. Amen.
ROBERT LOUIS STEVENSON

EXPECTANCY

God requires you to live in a state of expectancy. For Christ has promised "that, if we ask any thing according to his will, he heareth us: and if we know that he hear us, whatsoever we ask, we know that we have the petitions that we desired of him" (1 John 5:14–15). So pray, look up, await, and expect His blessings.

Beware in your prayers, above everything else, of limiting God, not only by unbelief, but by fancying that you know what He can do.
ANDREW MURRAY

Teach us, O gracious Lord, to begin our daily tasks with fear, to go on with obedience, and to finish them in love, and then to wait patiently in hope, and with cheerful confidence to look up to thee, whose promises are faithful and rewards infinite; through Jesus Christ our Lord.
GEORGE HICKES

I will look unto the LORD; I will wait for the God
of my salvation: my God will hear me.
MICAH 7:7

Lord, behold us here assembled. We thank Thee
for this place in which we dwell; for the love that
unites us; for the peace accorded us this day; for
the hope with which we expect the morrow; for the
health, the work, the food, and the bright skies, that
make our lives delightful; for our friends in all parts
of the earth. Let peace abound in our community.
Purge out of every heart the lurking grudge. Give
us grace and strength to forbear and to persevere.
Offenders, give us the grace to forgive offenders.
Forgetful ourselves, help us to bear cheerfully the
forgetfulness of others. Give us courage
and gaiety and the quiet mind.
ROBERT LOUIS STEVENSON

Our heavenly Father. . . We desire to go out today under Your eye and to keep close to You all the time. Show us the way, for we cannot find it ourselves, and could never get home without Your guidance. Put good thoughts into our hearts, for we can think beautiful thoughts only when they first drop from Heaven, like stars, and begin to glow in us! Every good thing comes down from above. As every stream is born in the skies, in the clouds—so every good thing in life is born in Heaven, comes out of Your very heart! Send down into our hearts, good and beautiful thoughts and feelings—that from our lives, may go divine blessings to all whom we come into contact with. . . . We ask all this in the name of Jesus Christ our Lord. Amen.

J. R. Miller

Attempt great things for God,
expect great things from God.
WILLIAM CAREY

Thou hast called us to Thyself, most merciful Father,
with love and with promises abundant; and we
are witnesses that it is not in vain that we draw
near to Thee. We bear witness to Thy faithfulness.
Thy promises are Yea and Amen. Thy blessings are
exceeding and abundant more than we know or
think. We thank Thee for the privilege of prayer,
and for Thine answers to prayer; and we rejoice that
Thou dost not answer according to our petitions.
We are blind, and are constantly seeking things
which are not best for us. If Thou didst grant all our
desires according to our requests, we should
be ruined. In dealing with our little children,
we give them, not the things which they ask for,
but the things which we judge to be best for
them; and Thou, our Father, art by Thy providence
overruling our ignorance and our headlong
mistakes, and are doing for us, not so much
the things that we request of Thee as the things
that we should ask; and we are, day by day,
saved from peril and from ruin by Thy better
knowledge and Thy careful love. Amen.
HENRY WARD BEECHER

FAITH

Faith is what moves mountains. Even faith as small as a mustard seed can uproot a mulberry tree and not just displace it—but plant it in the sea! "Faith is the substance of things hoped for, the evidence of things not seen" (Hebrews 11:1). Need more faith? Go to God. He'll give you as much as you need.

You can't know, you can only believe—or not.
C. S. LEWIS

Behold, Lord, an empty vessel that needs to be filled. My Lord, fill it. I am weak in the faith; strengthen me. I am cold in love; warm me and make me fervent, that my love may go out to my neighbor. I do not have a strong and firm faith; at times I doubt and am unable to trust You altogether. O Lord, help me. Strengthen my faith and trust in You.
MARTIN LUTHER

O God, teach me to breathe deeply in faith.
SØREN KIERKEGAARD

Almighty God, Lord of the storm and of the calm,
the vexed sea and the quiet haven, of day and of
night, of life and of death—grant unto us so to
have our hearts stayed upon Thy faithfulness, Thine
unchangingness and love, that, whatsoever betide
us, however black the cloud or dark the night, with
quiet faith trusting in Thee, we may look upon
Thee with untroubled eye, and walking in lowliness
toward Thee, and in lovingkindness toward one
another, abide all storms and troubles of this mortal
life, beseeching Thee that they may turn to the
soul's true good. We ask it for Thy mercy's sake,
shown in Jesus Christ our Lord. Amen.
GEORGE DAWSON

Lord, I will believe; I do believe.
HANNAH WHITALL SMITH

We desire, O Lord, that You will, to all Your other mercies, add that gift by which we shall trust in You—faith that works by love; faith that abides with us; faith that transforms material things, and gives them to us in spiritual meanings; faith that illumines the world by a light that never sets, that shines brighter than the day, and that clears the night quite out of our experience. . . . We beg You to grant us this faith, that shall give us victory over the world and over ourselves; that shall make us valiant in all temptation and bring us off conquerors and more than conquerors through Him that loved us. Amen.

HENRY WARD BEECHER

God, thou art Love.
I build my faith on that!
ROBERT BROWNING

FEAR

Even when Jesus was physically in their midst, the disciples cried out in fear. His response: "It is I; be not afraid" (John 6:20). Then, when they willingly let Him into their vessel, they immediately arrived at their destination. So don't let fear override you. Instead, cry out to Jesus in the midst of it and trust Him. In so doing, you'll end up where He wants you to be!

Every fear is distrust,
and trust is the remedy for fear.
A. B. SIMPSON

O Lord, my God, be not Thou far from me; my God, have regard to help me, for there have risen up against me sundry thoughts, and great fears, afflicting my soul. How shall I pass through unhurt? How shall I break them to pieces? This is my hope, my one only consolation, to flee unto Thee in every tribulation, to trust in Thee, to call upon Thee from my inmost heart, and to wait patiently for Thy consolation. Amen.
THOMAS Á KEMPIS

Eternal God, who commits to us the swift and solemn trust of life: since we know not what a day may bring forth, but only that the hour for serving You is always present, may we wake to Your instant claims, not waiting for tomorrow, but yielding today. Lay to rest the resistance of our passion, indolence, or fear. Consecrate the way our feet may go, and the humblest work will shine, and the roughest places be made plain. Lift us above unrighteous anger and mistrust into faith and hope and charity, through steady reliance on You. So may we be modest in our time of wealth, patient under disappointment, ready for danger, serene in death. In all things, draw us to Yourself that Your lost image may be traced again, and we may be at one with You.

JAMES MARTINEAU

Most loving Lord, give me a childlike love of Thee, which may cast out all fear. Amen.

EDWARD B. PUSEY

Lord of great compassion, we pray You for those who are nervously ill, and too weak and anxious to lift themselves above the fear and sadness that threaten to overwhelm them. Do You Yourself, O Lord, lift them up and deliver them, as You delivered Your disciples in the storm at sea, strengthening their faith and banishing their fear. Turning to You, O Lord, may they find You, and finding You may they find also all You have laid up for them within the fortress of Your love.

Elizabeth Goudge

Eternal God, lead us into the blessedness of the mystery of communion with Thee. Bow our spirits in deepest reverence before Thee, yet uplift us into a sense of kinship. Send the spirit of Thy Son into our hearts, crying "Abba, Father," that all unworthy fear may be banished by the gladness of Thy perfect love .... Touch us, O our Father, with a feeling of Thy great realities, for though our thought about Thee is better than our words, our experience of Thee is better than our thought.

Samuel McComb

FORGIVENESS

Someone once said that "Not forgiving someone is like drinking poison and expecting the other person to die." But that's no way to live. God has forgiven you on the condition that you forgive others. Live to forgive—today.

Our forgiving love toward men is the evidence of God's forgiving love in us. It is a necessary condition of the prayer of faith.
ANDREW MURRAY

Lord, You have plainly told me that all vengeance is Thine, not my business at all. You have said that I must forgive. I am willing to, but I've tried over and over, and the resentments keep surging back. Now I will this bitterness over to You. Here—I hold it out to You in my open hand. I promise only that I will not again close my fist and reclaim the resentment. Now I ask You to take it and handle these emotions that I cannot handle.
CATHERINE MARSHALL
Beyond Ourselves, p. 63

O Lord, because we often sin and have to ask for pardon, help us to forgive as we would be forgiven; neither mentioning old offenses committed against us, nor dwelling upon them in thought, but loving our brother freely as You freely love us; for Your name's sake.

CHRISTINA ROSSETTI

If my soul has turned perversely to the dark;
If I have left some brother wounded by the way;
If I have preferred my aims to Thine;
If I have been impatient and would not wait;
If I have marred the pattern drawn out for my life;
If I have cost tears to those I loved;
If my heart has murmured against Thy will,
O Lord, forgive.

F. B. MEYER

I offer to Thee prayers for the pardon of those especially, who have in any way injured, grieved or reproached me; or have caused me any harm or annoyance. And I offer also for all those whom I have in any way grieved, vexed, oppressed, and scandalized, by word or deed, knowingly or unknowingly; that Thou mayest equally forgive us all our sins, and all our offenses against each other. Take away, O Lord, from our hearts all suspiciousness, indignation, anger, and contention, and whatever is calculated to wound charity, and to lessen brotherly love. . . . Amen.

THOMAS Á KEMPIS

O Almighty God, give to Thy servant a meek and gentle spirit, that I may be slow to anger, and easy to mercy and forgiveness. Give me a wise and constant heart, that I may never be moved to an intemperate anger for any injury that is done or offered. Lord, let me ever be courteous, and easy to be entreated; let me never fall into a peevish or contentious spirit, but follow peace with all men; offering forgiveness, inviting them by courtesies, ready to confess my own errors, apt to make amends, and desirous to be reconciled. . . . In all things make me like unto the holy Jesus. Amen.

JEREMY TAYLOR

FRIENDSHIP

God would have you befriend all whom you meet, loving them, perhaps even laying down your life for them. May you meet others with the intention of being as good a friend to them as Jesus is to you, putting their needs and wants above your own.

It is very proper for friends,
when they part, to part with prayer.
MATTHEW HENRY

It is my joy in life to find
At every turning of the road,
The strong arm of a comrade kind
To help me onward with my load.
And since I have no gold to give,
And love alone must make amends,
My only prayer is, while I live,—
God make me worthy of my friends!
FRANK DEMPSTER SHERMAN

O blessed Lord and Savior, who hast commanded
us to love one another, grant us grace that, having
received Thine undeserved bounty, we may love
every man in Thee and for Thee. We implore Thy
clemency for all; but especially for the friends
whom Thy love has given to us. Love Thou them,
O Thou fountain of love, and make them to love
Thee with all their heart, with all their mind, and
with all their soul, that those things only which
are pleasing to Thee they may will, and speak, and
do. And though our prayer is cold, because our
charity is so little fervent, yet Thou art rich in mercy.
Measure not to them Thy goodness by the dullness
of our devotion; but as Thy kindness surpasseth
all human affection, so let Thy hearing transcend
our prayer. Do Thou that they, being always
and everywhere ruled and protected by Thee,
may attain in the end to everlasting life; and to
Thee, with the Father and the Holy Spirit, be all
honor and praise for ever and ever. Amen.
SAINT ANSELM

Almighty and most merciful Father, who has given
us a new commandment that we should love one
another, give us also grace that we may fulfill it.
Make us gentle, courteous, and forbearing. Direct
our lives so that we may look each to the good
of others in word and deed. And hallow all our
friendships by the blessing of Thy spirit, for His
sake, who loveth us and gave Himself for us,
Jesus Christ our Lord. Amen.
BROOKE FOSS WESTCOTT

Once more a new day lies before us, our Father. As we go out among men to do our work, touching the hands and lives of our fellows, make us, we pray Thee, friends of all the world. Save us from blighting the fresh flower of any heart by the flare of sudden anger or secret hate. May we not bruise the rightful self-respect of any by contempt or malice. Help us to cheer the suffering by our sympathy, to freshen the drooping by our hopefulness, and to strengthen in all the wholesome sense of worth and the joy of life. Save us from the deadly poison of class-pride. Grant that we may look all men in the face with the eyes of a brother. If any one needs us, make us ready to yield our help ungrudgingly, unless higher duties claim us, and may we rejoice that we have it in us to be helpful to our fellow men.

WALTER RAUSCHENBUSCH

I shook hands with my friend, Lord, and suddenly when I saw his sad and anxious face, I feared that You were not in his heart. I am troubled as I am before a closed tabernacle when there is no light to show that You are there. If You were not there, Lord, my friend and I would be separated. For His hand in mine would be only flesh in flesh and his love for me that of man for man. I want Your life for him as well as for me. For it is only in You that he can be my brother.

MICHEL QUOIST

GOD

God is the all in all. The air you breathe. The beauty you see. The splendor that surrounds you. The still, small voice within you. Make room for Him in your life. Be aware of Him every moment of your day. In doing so, may you become a beacon of light, directing others to the power behind all creation.

How few men are strong enough to be able
to endure silence. For in silence God
is speaking to the inner ear.
S. D. GORDON

Father in heaven, when the thought of You wakes
in our hearts, let it not wake like a frightened
bird that flies about in dismay, but like a child
waking from sleep with a heavenly smile.
SØREN KIERKEGAARD

God, this word we call You by is almost dead
and meaningless, transient and empty like all the
words men use. We ask You to renew its force and
meaning, to make it once again a name that brings
Your promise to us. Make it a living word which
tells us that You will be for us as You have always
been—trustworthy and hidden and very
close to us, Our God, now and forever.
HUUB OOSTERHUIS

Thou takest the pen—and the lines dance.
Thou takest the flute—and the notes shimmer.
Thou takest the brush—and the colors sing.
So all things have meaning and beauty
in that space beyond time where Thou art.
How, then, can I hold back anything from Thee?
DAG HAMMARSKJÖLD

Lord, may we love all Your creation, all the earth
and every grain of sand in it. May we love every leaf,
every ray of Your light. May we love the animals:
You have given them the rudiments of thought
and joy untroubled. Let us not trouble it; let us
not harass them, let us not deprive them of their
happiness, let us not work against Your intent.
For we acknowledge unto You that all is like an
ocean, all is flowing and bending, and that to
withhold any measure of love from anything
in Your universe is to withhold that
same measure from You.

FYODOR DOSTOEVSKY
adapted from passage in *The Brothers Karamazov*

God be in [my] head and in my understanding;
God be in my eyes and in my looking;
God be in my mouth and in my speaking;
God be in my heart and in my thinking;
God be at my end and at my departing.

OLD SARUM PRAYER

Lord, make me like crystal that
Your light may shine through me.

KATHERINE MANSFIELD

GOD'S PRESENCE

God's presence is everywhere—within and without. He is just waiting for His children to acknowledge Him, to see Him, to lean against His chest, to feel His breath. Take a moment today to recognize Him, to bow to His glowing presence, to be His willing vessel.

Always, everywhere God is present, and always seeks to discover Himself to each one.
A. W. TOZER

Lord, catch me off guard today. Surprise me with some moment of beauty or pain so that for at least a moment I may be startled into seeing that You are with me here in all Your splendor, always and everywhere, barely hidden, beneath, beyond, within this life I breathe.
FREDERICK BUECHNER

God, we thank You for the inspiration of Jesus.
Grant that we will love You with all our hearts,
souls, and minds, and love our neighbors as we love
ourselves, even our enemy neighbors. And we ask
You, God, in these days of emotional tension, when
the problems of the world are gigantic in extent
and chaotic in detail, to be with us in our going out
and our coming in, in our rising up and in our lying
down, in our moments of joy and in our moments
of sorrow, until the day when there shall
be no sunset and no dawn. Amen.

MARTIN LUTHER KING JR.

O eternal Light, shine into our hearts; eternal
Goodness, deliver us from evil; eternal Power, be
Thou our support; eternal Wisdom, scatter our
ignorance; eternal Pit, have mercy upon us. Grant
that with all our heart and mind and soul and
strength we may seek Thy face, and finally bring
us, by Thine infinite mercy, to Thy holy presence,
through Jesus Christ our Lord. Amen.

ALCUIN

O Lord, when I awake and day begins,
waken me to Thy Presence;
waken me to Thine indwelling;
waken me to inward sight of Thee,
and speech with Thee,
and strength from Thee;
that all my earthly walk may waken into song
and my spirit leap up to Thee all day, all ways.
ERIC MILNER-WHITE

Lord, You are closer to me
than my own breathing,
nearer than my hands and feet.
SAINT TERESA OF AVILA

GOD'S WILL

There is nothing so sweet as surrendering to God's will. For it takes all the pressure off of what you should or shouldn't do! So, allow God to be the Master Potter, to shape you into the beautiful vessel He has created you to be, to perform that which He has called you to do.

For each one of us, there is only one thing necessary: to fulfill our own destiny, according to God's will, to be what God wants us to be.
THOMAS MERTON

Lord, I am not yet willing for Thee to have Thy way with me, but I am willing to be made willing.
F. B. MEYER

I leave myself, Father, in Thy hands; make and remake this clay, shape it or grind it to atoms; it is Thine own, it has nought to say; only let it always be subservient to Thine ever-blessed designs, and let nothing in me oppose Thy good pleasure for which I was created. Require, command, forbid; what wouldst Thou have me do? what not do? Exalted, or abased, rejoicing or suffering, doing Thy work or laid aside, I will always praise Thee alike, ever yielding up all my own will to Thine! Nothing remains for me but to adopt the language of Mary: "Be it unto me according to thy words" (Luke 1:38).

FRANCOIS FÉNELON

Oh, Lord, bend me!

EVAN ROBERTS

Dear Lord, quiet my spirit and fix my thoughts on Thy will, that I may see what Thou wouldst have done, and contemplate its doing without self-consciousness or inner excitement, without haste and without delay, without fear of other people's judgments or anxiety about success, knowing only that it is Thy will and therefore must be done quietly, faithfully and lovingly, for in Thy will alone is our peace.

GEORGE APPLETON

O Lord, help us to go out of ourselves, so that we may give ourselves over to Thee, with all our powers, with all that we are and all that we have.

JACOB BOEHME

God's Word

God's word is filled with the wisdom, light, and love you need to get through this life—and to attain the crown of heaven. Feeling alone, lost, abandoned, confused, distraught, afraid? Dig into God's Word, follow its wisdom, perform its precepts, and you'll find the solace, strength, and solutions you seek.

> The word of God is the food by which
> prayer is nourished and made strong.
> E. M. Bounds

We most humbly beg you to give us grace not only to be hearers of the Word, but doers also of the same; not only to love, but also to live Your gospel; not only to favor, but also to follow Your godly doctrine; not only to profess, but also to practice Your blessed commandments, to the honor of Your Holy Name, and the health of our souls.
Thomas Becon

O God, whose name is holy of itself, we pray that
it may be hallowed also by us. To this end help us,
O blessed Father in heaven, that Thy word may
be taught in truth and purity, and that we, as Thy
children, may lead holy lives in accordance with it;
through Jesus Christ, Thy Son, our Lord. Amen.
MARTIN LUTHER

O Lord, heavenly Father, in whom is the fullness
of light and wisdom, enlighten our minds by Your
Holy Spirit, and give us grace to receive Your Word
with reverence and humility, without which no one
can understand Your truth. For Christ's sake, amen.
JOHN CALVIN

As we read Your word, may its lessons be made plain to us. Help us to receive its instruction into our hearts, so that our lives shall be controlled by it. As we pray, may Heaven's blessings be given to us: comfort for our sorrow, strength for our weakness, guidance for our feet, and wisdom for our ignorance. As we seek to be a blessing to others— may we receive the mind that was in Christ Jesus. We ask all in Jesus' precious name. Amen.

J. R. MILLER

Lord God, let us keep Your Scriptures in mind and meditate on them day and night, persevering in prayer; always on the watch. We beg You, Lord, to give us real knowledge of what we read and to show us not only how to understand it, but how to put it into practice, so that we may deserve to obtain spiritual grace, enlightened by the law of the Holy Spirit, through Jesus Christ our Lord, whose power and glory will endure throughout all ages.

ORIGEN

GRACE

Let's face it. No one is perfect by a long shot. But that's where God's grace comes in, saving you from what you once were, accepting you for what you are now, and giving you hope that you will someday become what God would have you be.

I am not what I ought to be, I am not what I want to be, I am not what I hope to be in another world; but still I am not what I once used to be, and by the grace of God I am what I am.

JOHN NEWTON

The things that we pray for, good Lord,
give us your grace to work for.
SIR THOMAS MORE

Grant us such grace that we may work Thy will,
And speak Thy words, and walk before Thy face,
Profound and calm like waters deep and still;
Grant us such grace.
CHRISTINA ROSSETTI

I come to Thee, O Lord, not only because I am
unhappy without thee; not only because I feel I
need thee, but because Thy grace draws me on to
seek Thee for Thy own sake, because Thou art so
glorious and beautiful. I come in great fear, but in
greater love. Oh may I never lose, as years pass away,
and the heart shuts up, and all things are a burden,
let me never lose this youthful, eager, elastic love of
Thee. Make Thy grace supply the failure of nature.
Do the more for me, the less I can do for myself.
JOHN HENRY NEWMAN

O my God, give me Thy grace so that the things of this earth and things more naturally pleasing to me, may not be as close as Thou art to me. Keep Thou my eyes, my ears, my heart from clinging to the things of this world. Break my bonds, raise my heart. Keep my whole being fixed on Thee. Let me never lose sight of Thee; and while I gaze on Thee, let my love of Thee grow more and more every day.
JOHN HENRY NEWMAN

Lord Jesus, merciful and patient, grant us grace, I beg You, ever to teach in the teachable spirit; learning along with those we teach, and learning from them whenever You please. Word of God, speak to us, speak by us what You will. Wisdom of God, instruct us...that we and they may all be taught of God.
CHRISTINA ROSSETTI

GRIEF

In the midst of immense sorrow, when your heart is weighed down by the heavy load of loss, there is one who has suffered as you are suffering. One who will sit and cry with you. One who will raise you up into His comforting arms. Seek Him now. Seek Him often. He will lead you out of the valley of darkness and into the sunshine of a new path.

Grief is like a long valley, a winding valley where any bend may reveal a totally new landscape.
C. S. LEWIS

Almighty God, grant unto us Thy love, that we may greatly rejoice; that we, knowing trouble, and acquainted with grief, may, through the goodly deliverance of faith and hope, come to the large joy of the peace that passeth all understanding. Amen.
GEORGE DAWSON

Lord, my loved ones are near me.
I know that they live in the shadow.
My eyes can't see them because they have left
for the moment their bodies as one
leaves behind outmoded clothing.
Their souls, deprived of their disguise,
no longer communicate with me.
But in You, Lord, I hear them calling me.
I see them beckoning to me.
I hear them giving me advice.
For they are now more vividly present.
Before, our bodies touched but not our souls.
Now I meet them when I meet You.
I receive them when I receive You.
I love them when I love You.
MICHEL QUOIST

O holy and loving Father, whose mercies are from
everlasting to everlasting, we thank Thee that Thy
children can flee for refuge in their afflictions to the
blessed certainty of Thy love. From every grief that
burdens our spirits, from the sense of solitude and
loss, from the doubt and fainting of the soul in its
trouble, we turn to Thee. Thou knowest our frame,
Thou rememberest that we are dust. Be Thou our
Strength and Deliverer; in our great need be Thou
our Helper; pour Thy consolations into our hearts,
and let the Gospel of Thy beloved Son minister
comfort and peace to our souls. Amen.
HENRY W. FOOTE

Gracious and most merciful God! Thou seest how my heart is filled with sorrow—a stone which I cannot throw off, a load of affliction too heavy to be borne, presses me to the earth—Therefore, I come to Thee, almighty God! I pour out my heart into Thy bosom, for those art my refuge and my salvation. I cast my troubles from myself upon Thee, and beseech thee to save and to assist me. The little bark, driven by fearful winds and waves, is held by the anchor; and so my soul clings to Thee, Thou living and almighty God. The timid roe pursued in the chase hastens to the mountains for deliverance, and I lift my eyes to Thee, my Rock, my Rescuer, and mighty Defender! I will not despair, for I know that Thou art an almighty God—Thou canst help me. O send deliverance now, and I am helped; speak but a single word, and my help has come.
JOHANN FRIEDRICH STARCK

Holy Father. . .we rejoice that we can turn to Thee in the midst of great anxiety, and commit all our troubles to Thy sure help. As Thou art with us in the sunlight, oh, be Thou with us in the cloud. In the path by which Thou guidest us, though it be through desert and stormy sea, suffer not our faith to fail, but sustain us by Thy near presence, and let the comforts which are in Jesus Christ fill our hearts with peace.
HENRY W. FOOTE

GUIDANCE

No matter where you are, you are never lost with God in your life. He is always with you, guiding you on the true path, a path unique to you and you alone. Your job is to merely look for His signposts, follow His directions, and trust that He knows your way.

If I have done anything in my life, it has been easy because the Master has gone before.
MARY SLESSOR

If I take the wings of the morning, and dwell in the uttermost parts of the sea; even there shall thy hand lead me, and thy right hand shall hold me.
PSALM 139:9–10

O Lord Jesus Christ, who art the Way, the Truth, and the Life, we pray Thee suffer us not to stray from Thee, who art the Way, nor to distrust Thee, who art the Truth, nor to rest in any other thing than Thee, who art the Life. Teach us, by Thy Holy Spirit what to believe, what to do, and wherein to take our rest. Amen.

ERASMUS

Lord, enable me to regulate this day so as to please You! Give me spiritual insight to discover what is Your will in all the relations of my life. Guide me as to my pursuits, my friendships, my reading, my dress, my Christian work.

HANNAH WHITALL SMITH

In me there is darkness,
But with Thee there is light,
I am lonely, but Thou leavest me not.
I am restless, but with Thee there is peace.
In me there is bitterness, but with Thee there is patience;
Thy ways are past understanding, but
Thou knowest the way for me.
DIETRICH BONHOEFFER

My Lord God, I have no idea where I am going.
I do not see the road ahead of me. I cannot know
for certain where it will end. Nor do I really know
myself, and the fact that I think that I am following
Your will does not mean that I am actually doing
so. But I believe that the desire to please You does
in fact please You. And I hope I have that desire
in all that I am doing. I hope that I will never do
anything apart from that desire. And I know that
if I do this You will lead me by the right road,
though I may know nothing about it. Therefore
will I trust you always, though I may seem to be
lost and in the shadow of death. I will not fear,
for You are ever with me, and You will
never leave me to face my perils alone.
THOMAS MERTON

HOLY SPIRIT

The Holy Spirit is the Wind and Breath that fills you, the invisible link connecting you to and helping you communicate with God. What you cannot express in words, He can make clear to the Father. For the Spirit is your Comforter, Helper, Encourager, Gift-Giver, and Guide. Open up and let Him in.

This thing of letting the Spirit teach must come
first in one's praying, and remain to the last,
and continue all along as the leading dominant
factor. He is a Spirit of prayer peculiarly.
S. D. GORDON

As the wind is Thy symbol so forward our goings.
As the dove so launch us heavenward.
As water so purify our spirits.
As a cloud so abate our temptation.
As dew so revive our languor.
As fire so purge out our dross.
CHRISTINA ROSSETTI

Creator Spirit, who broodest everlastingly over
the lands and waters of the earth, enduing them
with forms and colors which no human skill
can copy, give me today, I beseech Thee, the
mind and heart to rejoice in Thy creation.

JOHN BAILLIE

These are the gifts I ask
Of Thee, Spirit serene;
Strength for the daily task,
Courage to face the road,
Good cheer to help me bear the traveler's load;
And for the hours that come between,
An inward joy in all things heard and seen.

HENRY VAN DYKE

O Thou Divine Spirit that, in all events in life, art knocking at the door of my heart, help me to respond to Thee. I would not be driven blindly as the stars over their courses. I would not be made to work out Thy will unwillingly, to fulfill Thy law unintelligently, to obey Thy mandates unsympathetically. I would take the events of my life as good and perfect gifts from Thee; I would receive even the sorrows of life as disguised gifts from Thee. I would have my heart open at all times to receive Thee—at morning, noon and night; in spring, and summer, and winter. Whether Thou comest to me in sunshine or in rain, I would take Thee into my heart joyfully. Thou art Thyself more than the sunshine; Thou art Thyself compensation for the rain; it is Thee and not Thy gifts I crave; knock, and I shall open unto Thee.

GEORGE MATHESON

Blessed Prayer-Spirit, Master-Spirit,
teach me how to pray.
S. D. GORDON

HOPE

Faith and hope are inextricably linked, for, as Hebrews 11:1 tells us, "Faith is the substance of things hoped for, the evidence of things not seen." So be constant in your faith, and you can be sure your hopes will one day rise up to become reality.

The word hope I take for faith; and indeed hope is nothing else but the constancy of faith.
JOHN CALVIN

O God, by whose command the order of time runs its course: Forgive, we pray thee, the impatience of our hearts; make perfect that which is lacking in our faith; and, while we tarry the fulfilment of Thy promises, grant us to have a good hope because of Thy word; through Jesus Christ our Lord.
SAINT GREGORY OF NAZIANZUS

Lord, perfect for me what is lacking in Thy gifts;
of faith, help Thou mine unbelief; of hope,
establish my trembling hope; of love,
kindle its smoking flax.
LANCELOT ANDREWES

O Christ, our Morning Star,
Splendor of Light Eternal,
shining with the glory of the rainbow,
come and waken us
from the greyness of our apathy
and renew in us Your gift of hope. Amen.
SAINT BEDE THE VENERABLE

O Christ, our only Savior, so dwell within us that we may go forth with the light of hope in our eyes, and the first of inspiration on our lips, Thy word on our tongue, and Thy love in our hearts: through Jesus Christ our Lord. Amen.

ANONYMOUS

Grant unto us, Almighty God, in all time of sore distress, the comfort of the forgiveness of our sins. In time of darkness give us blessed hope, in time of sickness of body give us quiet courage; and when the heart is bowed down, and the soul is very heavy, and life is a burden, and pleasure a weariness, and the sun is too bright, and life too mirthful, then may that Spirit, the Spirit of the Comforter, come upon us, and after our darkness may there be the clear shining of the heavenly light; that so, being uplifted again by Thy mercy, we may pass on through this our mortal life with quiet courage, patient hope, and unshaken trust, hoping through Thy loving-kindness and tender mercy to be delivered from death into the large life of the eternal years. Hear us of Thy mercy, through Jesus Christ our Lord. Amen.

GEORGE DAWSON

Jesus Christ

Jesus Christ is the person of God who came to earth to save us by showing us the Way, the Truth, and the Life. He is the breaker of the barrier our faults and failings have erected between us and God. Oh, what a Savior! Because of Him, we can boldly break through in prayer!

Prayer is the risen Jesus coming in with His resurrection power, given free rein in our lives, and then using His authority to enter any situation and change things.
OLE HALLESBY

Lord Jesus, may the sweet burning ardor of Your love so absorb my soul entirely and make it a stranger to all that is not You or for You.
SAINT FRANCIS OF ASSISI

I thank Thee, Savior,
because Thou has died for me.
OLE HALLESBY

Be born in us
Incarnate Love
take our flesh and blood and
give us Your humanity;
take our eyes and
give us Your vision;
take our minds and
give us Your pure thought;
take our feet and
set them in Your path;
take our hands and
fold them in Your prayer;
take our hearts and
give them Your will to Love.
CARYLL HOUSELANDER

O beloved Savior, show Yourself to us who knock,
that knowing You, we may love You alone, desire
only You, think always of You alone, meditating day
and night on Your words. Awaken in us such a love
as may be rightly and fittingly rendered to You.
O God, may Your love take possession of our
whole being and make it totally Yours.

SAINT COLUMBANUS

O most merciful Redeemer, Friend and Brother,
May I know Thee more clearly,
Love Thee more dearly,
Follow Thee more nearly, day by day.

SAINT RICHARD OF CHICHESTER

JOY

Whereas happiness is based on events or happenings in the material world, joy goes much deeper. It's a gladness and calm assurance that in spite of what is happening all around you, Jesus is walking by your side, the Holy Spirit is filling you from within, and God is working all things out for your good. That's a bubbling-over joy that can never be taken away.

It is pleasing to the dear God whenever thou rejoicest or laughest from the bottom of thy heart.
MARTIN LUTHER

Grant me, O Lord, the royalty of inward happiness and the serenity which comes from living close to Thee. Daily renew the sense of joy, and let the eternal spirit of the Father dwell in my soul and body, filling every corner of my heart with light and grace, so that bearing about with me the infection of a good courage, I may be a diffuser of life and may meet all ills and crosses with gallant and high-hearted happiness, giving Thee thanks always for all things.
ROBERT LOUIS STEVENSON

Cheerfully may we go in the road which Thou has marked out, not desiring too earnestly that it should be either more smooth or wise; but daily seeking our way by Thy light, may we trust ourselves and the issue of our journey to Thee, the Fountain of Joy, and sing songs of praise as we go along. Then, O Lord, receive us at the gate of life which Thou has opened for us in Christ Jesus. Amen.

JAMES MARTINEAU

Grant me, even me, my dearest Lord, to know Thee, and love Thee, and rejoice in Thee. And if I cannot do these perfectly in this life, let me at least advance to higher degrees every day, till I can come to do them in perfection. Let the knowledge of Thee increase in me here, that it may be full hereafter. Let the love of Thee grow every day more and more here, that it may be perfect hereafter; that my joy may be great in itself, and full in Thee. I know, O God, that Thou art a God of truth. O make good Thy gracious promises to me, that my joy may be full. Amen.

SAINT AUGUSTINE

O Thou, who art the true Sun of the world, ever rising, and never going down; who, by Thy most wholesome appearing and sight dost nourish, and gladden all things in heaven and earth; we beseech Thee mercifully to shine into our hearts, that the night and darkness of sin, and the mists of error on every side, being driven away, by the brightness of Thy shining within our hearts, we may all our life walk without stumbling, as in the daytime, and, being pure and clean from the works of darkness, may abound in all good works which Thou hast prepared for us to walk in. Amen.

Erasmus

Come and help us, Lord Jesus. A vision of Your face will brighten us; but to feel Your Spirit touching us will make us vigorous. Oh! for the leaping and walking of the man born lame. May we today dance with holy joy, like David before the ark of God. May a holy exhilaration take possession of every part of us; may we be glad in the Lord; may our mouth be filled with laughter, and our tongue with singing, "for the Lord hath done great things for us whereof we are glad."

Charles Spurgeon

LOVE

Love is the most powerful force in the world because God is Love—and Jesus is Love personified. There is nothing deeper, wider, longer, or higher than the love Christ has for you. Nor can anything separate you from that love. And you have the privilege of showing that love to others. May God increase your love divine.

To love someone means to see him
as God intended him.
FYODOR DOSTOEVSKY

Fill us, we pray, Lord, with Your light and life that we may show forth Your wondrous glory. Grant that Your love may so fill our lives that we may count nothing too small to do for You, nothing too much to give and nothing too hard to bear.
SAINT IGNATIUS OF LOYOLA

Lord Jesus Christ, that our prayer may be rightly directed, we pray first for one all important need. Help us to love You, increase our love, inflame it. This prayer You will surely hear, for You are not love of a crude selfish sort, merely an uncaring object of regard. If You were You would not be the love that casts out all fear. No, You are a compassionate love; more than that You are love of such a sort that draws out the love that loves You, nurturing and encouraging us to increase daily in Your love. Love divine, increase our love.

SØREN KIERKEGAARD

Grant that with Your love, I may be big enough to reach the world, and small enough to be one with You.

MOTHER TERESA

You who are love itself,
give me the grace of love,
give me Yourself,
so that all my days may finally empty
into the one day of Your eternal life.
KARL RAHNER

O God, Fountain of love, pour Thy love into our
souls, that we may love those whom Thou lovest,
with the love Thou givest us, and think and speak of
them tenderly, meekly, lovingly; and so loving our
brethren and sisters for Thy sake, may grow in
Thy love, and dwelling in love may dwell in
Thee; for Jesus Christ's sake. Amen.
EDWARD B. PUSEY

OBEDIENCE

God requires your obedience. Not because He wants to make life difficult for you, but because He alone knows what's good for you. In fact, when you live in obedience, you find yourself enjoying all that God has planned for you. Whether or not you think, from your limited knowledge and perspective, what He's telling you makes sense, you can trust the Father truly knows best.

> One act of obedience is better
> than one hundred sermons.
> DIETRICH BONHOEFFER

Make us of quick understanding and tender conscience, O Lord; that understanding, we may obey every word of Thine this day, and discerning, may follow every suggestion of Thine indwelling Spirit. Speak, Lord, for Thy servant heareth, through Jesus Christ our Lord. Amen.
CHRISTINA ROSSETTI

Almighty and everlasting God, only speak to us that we may hear Thee. Then speak to us again and yet again so that when in our hearts we answer Thee by saying No, we may at least know well to whom we say it, and what it costs us to say it, and what it costs our brothers, and what it costs Thee. And when at those moments that we can never foretell we say Yes to Thee, forgive our halfheartedness, accept us as we are, work Thy miracle within us, and of Thy grace give us strength to follow wherever love may lead.

FREDERICK BUECHNER

Almighty God, who art over all things, Life of all life—stir in our souls, that we, being moved by Thy Spirit, may see those things which are fairest and truest in life, and clinging thereunto, be enabled to get the victory over that which is mean and base; that so at last, all evil passion and unholy desire, all self-will and contrariness to Thee, may be overcome, and we come at last to that sublime state of willing obedience, when Thy will shall be in us supreme. Of Thy mercy hear us, through Jesus Christ our Lord. Amen.

GEORGE DAWSON

From this moment on I promise that I'll try to do whatever You tell me for the rest of my life, insofar as You'll make it clear to me what Your wishes are. I'm weak and many times I'll probably want to renege on this. But Lord, You'll have to help me with that, too.

CATHERINE MARSHALL
Beyond Ourselves, p. 43

Make us remember, O God, that every day is Your gift, to be used according to Your command.

SAMUEL JOHNSON

PATIENCE

The rewards of waiting on God with courage and patience are not only gaining God's ear, but securing His salvation, strength, protection, help, peace, mercy, wisdom, the earth as your inheritance, and the expected answers to your prayers. It pays to persistently practice patience.

It is hard to wait and press and pray,
and hear no voice, but stay till God answers.
E. M. BOUNDS

Gracious and Holy Father, please give me: intellect to understand You, reason to discern You, diligence to seek You, wisdom to find You, a spirit to know You, a heart to meditate upon You, ears to hear You, eyes to see You, a tongue to proclaim You, a way of life pleasing to You, patience to wait for You and perseverance to look for You. Grant me a perfect end, Your holy presence, a blessed resurrection and life everlasting.
SAINT BENEDICT OF NURSIA

God, teach me to be patient, teach me to go slow, teach me how to wait on You when my way I do not know. Teach me sweet forbearance when things do not go right so I remain unruffled when others grow uptight. Teach me how to quiet my racing, rising heart so I might hear the answer You are trying to impart. Teach me to let go, dear God, and pray undisturbed until my heart is filled with inner peace and I learn to know Your will.

HELEN STEINER RICE

Every time I do not behave like a donkey, it is the worse for me. How does a donkey behave? If it is slandered, it keeps silent; if it is not fed, it keeps silent; if it is forgotten, it keeps silent; it never complains, however much it is beaten or ill-used, because it has a donkey's patience. That is how the servant of God must be. I stand before you, Lord, like a donkey.

SAINT PETER CLAVER

O God, who makest cheerfulness the companion
of strength, but apt to take wings in time of sorrow,
we humbly beseech Thee that if, in Thy sovereign
wisdom, Thou sendest weakness, yet for Thy mercy's
sake deny us not the comfort of patience. Lay not
more upon us to bear; and, since the fretfulness
of our spirit is more hurtful than the heaviness of
our burden, grant us that heavenly calmness
which comes of owning Thy hand in all things,
and patience in the trust that Thou
doest all things well. Amen.
ROWLAND WILLIAMS

Take from us, O God, all tediousness
of spirit, all impatience and unquietness.
Let us possess ourselves in patience:
through Jesus Christ our Lord.
JEREMY TAYLOR

PEACE

Although you may not be able to control what happens in the outer world, you can take steps to assure peace in your inner world. And it all begins with your seeking out God. It is through Him you may gain access to that peace beyond all understanding. That peace that ripples out to those around you.

Peace begins with a smile.
MOTHER TERESA

Lord, make me an instrument of Your peace. Where there is hatred, let me sow love; where there is injury, pardon; where there is doubt, faith; where there is despair, hope; where there is darkness, light; where there is sadness, joy. O Divine Master, grant that I may not so much seek to be consoled as to console; to be understood as to understand; to be loved as to love. For it is in giving that we receive; it is in pardoning that we are pardoned; and it is in dying that we are born to eternal life.
SAINT FRANCIS OF ASSISI

God grant me the serenity
to accept the things I cannot change;
Courage to change the things I can;
And wisdom to know the difference.
Living one day at a time;
Enjoying one moment at a time;
Accepting hardships as the pathway to peace;
Taking, as He did, this sinful world as it is,
not as I would have it;
Trusting that He will make all things
right if I surrender to His will;
That I may be reasonably happy in this life
and supremely happy with Him forever in the next.
REINHOLD NIEBUHR

Almighty God, the Refuge of all that are
distressed, grant unto us that, in all trouble of this
our mortal life, we may flee to the knowledge of Thy
lovingkindness and tender mercy; that so, sheltering
ourselves therein, the storms of life may pass
over us, and not shake the peace of God
that is within us. . . . Amen.
GEORGE DAWSON

Grant us, O Lord, the blessing of those whose minds are stayed on You, so that we may be kept in perfect peace: a peace which cannot be broken. Let not our minds rest upon any creature, but only upon the Creator; not upon goods, things, houses, lands, inventions or vanities, or foolish fashions, lest, our peace being broken, we become cross and brittle and given over to envy. From all such deliver us, O God, and grant us Your peace.
GEORGE FOX

O Lord, calm the waves of this heart; calm its tempest! Calm thyself, O my soul, so that the divine can act in thee! Calm thyself, O my soul, so that God is able to repose in thee, so that His peace may cover thee! Yes, Father in heaven, often have we found that the world cannot give us peace. O but make us feel that Thou art able to give peace; let us know the truth of Thy promise: that the whole world may not be able to take away Thy peace.
SØREN KIERKEGAARD

PLANS

Your plans, which are usually based on following the desires of your heart, are one thing. But God's plans for you may be another thing altogether. The idea is to home in on the wisdom of God's plans, making sure your desires have fused with His. For if you long and love to be in Him, filling the desire of His heart, He will give you the desires of your heart (see Psalm 37:4).

If God is your partner, make your plans BIG!
D. L. MOODY

O God, grant that at all times You may find me
as You desire me and where You would have me
be, that You may lay hold on me fully, both by the
Within and the Without of myself, grant that I may
never break this double thread of my life.
TEILHARD DE CHARDIN

O Lord, let nothing divert our advance toward You, but in this dangerous labyrinth of the world and the whole course of our pilgrimage here, Your heavenly dictates be our map and Your holy life be our guide.
JOHN WESLEY

We beseech Thee, O Lord, to enlighten our minds and to strengthen our wills, that we may know what we ought to do, and be enabled to do it, through the grace of Thy most Holy Spirit, and for the merits of Thy Son, Jesus Christ our Lord.
WILLIAM BRIGHT

Dear God, You choose. I choose what You choose.
S. D. GORDON

O God, who puttest into our hearts such deep
desire, that we cannot be at peace until we enjoy
the feeling of Thy love; mercifully grant that the
unspeakable sighing of our souls' need may not go
unsatisfied because of any unrighteousness of heart,
which must divide us from the All-holy One; but
strengthen us to do right by whomsoever we have
wronged in thought, word, or deed; to renounce all
plans of wrongdoing for the future; to purify our
thoughts and govern our appetites, so that we may
have no bar between us and Thy glory, but enjoy
Thy peace which passeth understanding. Amen.
ROWLAND WILLIAMS

PRAISE

When you lift your eyes up to God and the heavenly realm, you are compelled to lift your voice in praise to Him, the Master of the Universe, for all blessings, seen and yet to be seen. So if you are ever down, look up—and you will be supernaturally lifted up in heart, soul, spirit, and mind.

Aim at heaven and you will get earth thrown in.
Aim at earth and you get neither.
C. S. LEWIS

Open wide the window of our spirits and fill us
full of light; open wide the door of our hearts,
that we receive and entertain Thee with all
our powers of adoration and love.
CHRISTINA ROSSETTI

O God our Father, we would thank Thee for all
the bright things of life. Help us to see them,
and to count them, and to remember them,
that our lives may flow in ceaseless praise;
for the sake of Jesus Christ our Lord.
JOHN HENRY JOWETT

O Lord, my God, for life and reason, nurture,
preservation, guidance, education; for Thy gifts of
grace and nature, for Thy calling, recalling, manifold
recalling me again and again, for Thy forbearance,
long-suffering, and long long-suffering toward me,
even until now; for all from whom I have received
any good or help; for the use of Thy present good
things; for Thy promise, and my hope, of good
things to come. For all these things and for all
other, which I know, which I know not, manifest
or secret, remembered or forgotten by me,
I praise Thee, I bless Thee, I give Thee thanks;
and I will praise, and bless, and give Thee
thanks all the days of my life.
LANCELOT ANDREWES

You awaken us to delight in Your praises;
for You made us for Yourself, and our
heart is restless until it reposes in You.
SAINT AUGUSTINE

It is in my heart to praise Thee, O my God;
Let me never forget Thee,
what Thou has been to me. . .
When the floods sought to sweep me away
Thou set a compass for them,
how far they should pass over;
When my way was through the sea,
and when I passed under the mountains
there was Thou present with me;
When the weight of the hills was upon me
Thou upheld me, else had I sunk under the earth;
When I was one altogether helpless,
when tribulation and anguish was upon me
day and night, and the earth was without
foundation; . . . Thou was with me and
the Rock of Thy Presence.
JAMES NAYLOR

PRAYER

There is nothing more powerful than prayer. And nothing more forceful than prayer that comes straight from the heart. God leans down, hears, and understands all that you want to say—with and without words. It's a mystery that leads you and your petitions ever upward.

We must begin to believe that God, in the mystery of prayer, has entrusted us with a force that can move the heavenly world, and can bring its power down to earth.
ANDREW MURRAY

After this manner therefore pray ye: Our Father which art in heaven, Hallowed be thy name. Thy kingdom come, Thy will be done in earth, as it is in heaven. Give us this day our daily bread. And forgive us our debts, as we forgive our debtors. And lead us not into temptation, but deliver us from evil: For thine is the kingdom, and the power, and the glory, for ever. Amen.
MATTHEW 6:9–13

Teach us, O Spirit of God, that silent language which says all things. Teach our souls to remain silent in Thy presence: that we may adore Thee in the depths of our being and await all things from thee, whilst asking of thee nothing but the accomplishment of Thy will. Teach us to remain quiet under Thy action and produce in our soul that deep and simple prayer which says nothing and expresses everything, which specifies nothing and includes everything.

JEAN NICHOLAS GROU

Lord, save us from being self-centered in our prayers and teach us to remember to pray for others. May we be so bound up in love with those for whom we pray, that we may feel their needs as acutely as our own, and intercede for them with sensitivity, with understanding and with imagination.

JOHN CALVIN

Assist me mercifully, O Lord, in all my supplications and prayers, that I may not draw near to Thee with my lips while my heart is far from Thee. Give me a hearty desire to pray, and grace to pray faithfully, that I may live under Thy most mighty protection here, and praise Thee hereafter; through Jesus Christ.

SABINE BARING-GOULD

O God, forgive the poverty, the pettiness, Lord, the childish folly of our prayers. Listen not to our words, but to the groanings that cannot be uttered; hearken, not to our petitions, but to the crying of our need. So often we pray for that which is already ours, neglected and unappropriated; so often for that which never can be ours; so often for that which we must win ourselves; and then labor endlessly for that which can only come to us in prayer. How often we have prayed for the coming of Thy kingdom, yet when it has sought to come through us we have sometimes barred the way; we have wanted it without in others, but not in our own hearts. We feel it is we who stand between man's need and Thee; between ourselves and what we might be; and we have no trust in our own strength, or loyalty, or courage. O give us to love Thy will, and seek Thy kingdom first of all. Sweep away our fears, our compromise, our weakness, lest at last we be found fighting against Thee. Amen.

WILLIAM EDWIN ORCHARD

PROTECTION

God is your refuge, your fortress. No evil can reach you when you abide in Him. From this place of safety, there is nothing God cannot do through, in, and with you. For it is in that place of confidence that you find the courage and strength to be whom He has called you to be.

I surround myself with the protection of Almighty God and in the name of Jesus Christ I say that nothing shall get through to hurt me.

AGNES SANFORD

Thank You, Lord Jesus,
that You will be our hiding place,
whatever happens.
CORRIE TEN BOOM

I arise today, through
God's strength to pilot me,
God's might to uphold me,
God's wisdom to guide me,
God's eye to look before me,
God's ear to hear me,
God's word to speak for me,
God's hand to guard me,
God's shield to protect me,
God's host to save me
From snares of devils,
From temptation of vices,
From everyone who shall wish me ill,
afar and near. . . .
Christ with me,
Christ before me,
Christ behind me,
Christ in me,
Christ beneath me,
Christ above me,
Christ on my right,
Christ on my left,
Christ when I lie down,
Christ when I sit down,
Christ when I arise,
Christ in the heart of every man who thinks of me,
Christ in the mouth of everyone who speaks of me,
Christ in every eye that sees me,
Christ in every ear that hears me.

SAINT PATRICK'S BREASTPLATE

O Lord, give us grace, I pray Thee, so to realize
Thine Almighty succor pledged to us,
Thy protecting Presence surrounding us,
Thine all-seeing eye fixed upon us, that we
may cease to tremble at man's anger, or shrink
from man's ridicule, but may with a good
courage perform the work Thou givest us to do.
CHRISTINA ROSSETTI

Dear God, be good to me;
The sea is so wide,
and my boat is so small.
PRAYER USED BY BRETON FISHERMEN

PURPOSE

When you allow God to have His way in you, when you are clear on what He would have your purpose be, and when you then live out your life as intended, you become the earthly conduit of God's heavenly blessings. In this way, your purpose becomes your pleasure.

Make sure you are doing what God wants you to do—then do it with all your strength.
GEORGE WASHINGTON

Use me then, my Savior, for whatever purpose, and in whatever way, Thou mayest require. Here is my poor heart, an empty vessel; fill it with Thy grace. Here is my sinful and troubled soul; quicken it and refresh it with Thy love. Take my heart for Thine abode; my mouth to spread abroad the glory of Thy name; my love and all my powers, for the advancement of believing people; and never suffer the steadfastness and confidence of my faith to abate—that so at all times I may be enabled from the heart to say, "Jesus needs me, and I Him."
D. L. MOODY

Search me, oh God, and know my heart and help
me know it; try me and know my innermost,
undermost thoughts and purposes and ambitions,
and help me know them; and see what way there be
in me that is a grief to Thee; and then lead me out
of that way unto Thy way, the way everlasting.
For Jesus' sake; aye for men's sake, too.
S. D. GORDON

O God, we thank You for the lives of great saints
and prophets in the past, who have revealed
to us that we can stand up amid the problems
and difficulties and trials of life and not give in.
We thank you for our foreparents, who've given
us something in the midst of the darkness of
exploitation and oppression to keep going. Grant
that we will go on with the proper faith and the
proper determination of will, so that we will be
able to make a creative contribution to this world.
In the name and spirit of Jesus we pray.
MARTIN LUTHER KING JR.

O Lord, I give myself to Thee, I trust Thee
wholly. Thou art wiser than I, more loving to me
than I myself. Deign to fulfill Thy high purposes in
me whatever they be; work in me and through me.
I am born to serve Thee, to be Thine, to be Thy
instrument. Let me be Thy blind instrument.
I ask not to see, I ask not to know,
I ask simply to be used. Amen.
JOHN HENRY NEWMAN

O Christ Jesus,
when all is darkness
and we feel our weakness and helplessness,
give us the sense of Your presence,
Your love, and Your strength.
Help us to have perfect trust
in Your protecting love
and strengthening power,
so that nothing may frighten or worry us,
for, living close to You,
we shall see Your hand,
Your purpose, Your will through all things.
SAINT IGNATIUS OF LOYOLA

Relationships

You are to do unto others as Christ does unto you. Forgive them, serve them, practice patience with them—treat them as you would have them treat you. But the greatest of these "treatments" is love. It's a tall order, but with God's strength, you can fill it.

> In the time we have it is surely our duty to
> do all the good we can to all the people
> we can in all the ways we can.
> WILLIAM BARCLAY

Give us patience and fortitude to put self aside
for You in the most unlikely people: to know that
every man's and any man's suffering is our own first
business, for which we must be willing to go out of
our way and to leave our own interests.
CARYLL HOUSELANDER

Grant me to recognize in other men,
Lord God, the radiance of Your own face.
TEILHARD DE CHARDIN

May I be no man's enemy, and may I be
the friend of that which is eternal and abides.
May I never quarrel with those nearest me;
and if I do, may I be reconciled quickly.
May I love, seek, and attain only that which is good.
May I wish for all men's happiness and envy none.
May I never rejoice in the ill-fortune
of one who has wronged me.
May I win no victory that harms
either me or my opponent.
May I reconcile friends who are
angry with one another.
May I, to the extent of my power, give all needful
help to my friends and all who are in want.
May I never fail a friend who is in danger.
May I respect myself.
May I always keep tame that which rages in me.
May I accustom myself to be gentle, and never be
angry with people because of circumstances.
May I never discuss who is wicked and what
wicked things he has done, but know good
people and follow in their footsteps.
EUSEBIUS OF CAESAREA

O God, You have bound us together in this
bundle of life; give us grace to understand how
our lives depend on the courage, the industry, the
honesty and integrity of our fellow men; that we
may be mindful of their needs, grateful for their
faithfulness, and faithful in our responsibilities
to them; through Jesus Christ our Lord.
REINHOLD NIEBUHR

O God of love, we pray Thee to give us love:
Love in our thinking, love in our speaking,
Love in our doing, and love in the
hidden places of our souls;
Love of our neighbours near and far;
Love of our friends, old and new;
Love of those with whom we find it hard to bear,
And love of those who find it hard to bear with us;
Love of those with whom we work,
And love of those with whom we take our ease;
Love in Joy, love in sorrow;
Love in life and love in death;
That so at length we may be worthy
to dwell with Thee,
Who art eternal love.
WILLIAM TEMPLE

RENEWAL

When you are dry of mind, thirsty of spirit, weary in body, parched of purpose, come. Come to the feet of your Creator, to the side of your Savior, and into the arms of the Spirit. There you will find the replenishment you need to not only survive—but thrive!

The bottle of the creature cracks and dries up,
but the well of the Creator never fails;
happy is he who dwells at the well.
CHARLES SPURGEON

Breathe on me, Breath of God,
Fill me with life anew,
That I may love what Thou dost love,
And do what Thou wouldst do.
EDWIN HATCH

O God our Father, who sent Your Son to be our Savior: renew in us day by day the power of your Holy Spirit; that with knowledge and zeal, with courage and love, with gratitude and hope, we may strive powerfully in Your service: may He keep our vision clear, our aspiration high, our purpose firm and our sympathy wide; that we may live as faithful soldiers and servants of our Lord Jesus Christ.

WILLIAM TEMPLE

Dear God, we are as strangers in Your wondrous universe, yet as children at home within Your shelter. You inspire joyful confidence in You. Enlightener of true seers and prophets, You are our Strength. May their faith and spirit rest upon all our life, refreshing the weariest task. In life and in death, You are the steadfast light of our hearts; You are our portion forever.

JAMES MARTINEAU

O Holy Spirit, Love of God, infuse Thy grace,
and descend plentifully into my heart; enlighten
the dark corners of this neglected dwelling, and
scatter there Thy cheerful beams; dwell in that soul
that longs to be Thy temple; water that barren soil,
overrun with weeds and briars, and lost for want of
cultivating, and make it fruitful with Thy dew from
heaven. O come, Thou refreshment of them that
languish and faint. Come, Thou Star and Guide of
them that sail in the tempestuous sea of the world;
Thou only Haven of the tossed and shipwrecked.
Come, Thou Glory and Crown of the living,
and only Safeguard of the dying. Come,
Holy Spirit, in much mercy, and make
me fit to receive Thee. Amen.
SAINT AUGUSTINE

You are the same yesterday, today, and forever;
and therefore, waiting on Thee Lord,
I trust that I shall at length renew my strength.
WILLIAM WILBERFORCE

REST

By resting in God, you find the renewed power you need to continue on in God's strength—not your own. It is the wise walker who takes time out to rest in Christ. For by doing so, such a traveler lessens the possibility of a misstep or stumble.

Rest time is not waste time. It is economy to gather fresh strength... It is wisdom to take occasional furlough. In the long run, we shall do more by sometimes doing less.
CHARLES SPURGEON

Come now, little one, turn aside for a while from your daily employment, escape for a moment from the tumult of your thoughts. Put aside your weighty cares, let your burdensome distractions wait, free yourself awhile for God and rest awhile in Him. Enter the inner chamber of your soul, shut out everything except God and that which can help you in seeking Him. And when you have shut the door, seek God. Now, my whole heart, say to God, "I seek Your face, Lord, it is Your face I seek."
SAINT ANSELM

O Omnipotent God, who cares for each of us as if
no one else existed and for all of us as if we were
all but one! Blessed is the person who loves You.
To You I entrust my whole being and all I have
received from You. You made me for Yourself,
and my heart is restless until it rests in You.
SAINT AUGUSTINE

Go with each of us to rest; if any awake, temper
them the dark hours of watching; and when the day
returns, return to us, our sun and comforter, and
call us up with morning faces and with morning
hearts, eager to labor, eager to be happy, if happiness
should be our portion, and if the day be marked
for sorrow, strong to endure it. Amen.
ROBERT LOUIS STEVENSON

O Lord, Thy hands have formed us, and Thou hast sent us into this world, that we may walk in the way that leads to heaven and Thyself, and may find a lasting rest in Thee, Who art the Source and Centre of our souls. Look in pity on us poor pilgrims in the narrow way; let us not go astray, but reach at last our true home where our Father dwells. Guide and govern us from day to day, and bestow on us food and strength for body and soul, that we may journey on in peace. Forgive us for having hitherto so often wavered or looked back, and let us hence-forward march straight on in the way of Thy laws, and may our last step be a safe and peaceful passage to the arms of Thy love, and the blessed fellowship of the saints in light. Hear us, O Lord, and glorify Thy name in us, that we may glorify Thee for ever and ever. Amen.

GERHARD TERSTEEGEN

O Lord, who art the shadow of a great rock in a weary land, who beholdest thy weak creatures, weary of labor, weary of pleasures, weary of heart from hope deferred, and weary of self. In Thine abundant compassion and unutterable tenderness bring us we pray Thee, unto Thy rest, through Jesus Christ, Thy Son, our Savior.

CHRISTINA ROSSETTI

SALVATION

You cannot in your own power save yourself. And why should you even try? For there is one so much greater—Christ—who has already done it for you. Like one who is drowning, your only job is to allow Him to pull you safely to shore.

Your salvation does not depend on what
you are but on what He is. For every look
at self, take ten looks at Christ.
F. B. MEYER

O God, our leader and our Master and our Friend, forgive our imperfections and our little motives, take us and make us one with Thy great purpose, use us and do not reject us, make us all servants of Thy kingdom, weave our lives into Thy struggle to conquer and to bring peace and union to the world. We are small and feeble creatures, we are feeble in speech, feebler still in action, nevertheless let but Thy light shine upon us, and there is not one of us who cannot be lit by Thy fire and who cannot lose himself in Thy salvation. Take us into Thy purposes, O God. Let Thy kingdom come into our hearts and into this world.
H. G. WELLS

O Lord, never suffer us to think that we can
stand by ourselves, and not need thee.
JOHN DONNE

We beseech Thee, Lord and Master, to be our
help and succor. Save those who are in tribulation;
have mercy on the lonely; lift up the fallen; show
Thyself unto the needy; heal the ungodly; convert
the wanderers of Thy people; feed the hungry; raise
up the weak; comfort the faint-hearted. Let all the
peoples know that Thou art God alone, and Jesus
Christ is Thy Son, and we are Thy people and
the sheep of Thy pasture; for the sake
of Christ Jesus. Amen.
SAINT CLEMENT OF ROME

In the confidence of Your goodness and great mercy,
O Lord, I draw to You, as a sick person to the healer,
as one hungry and thirsty to the fountain of life, a
creature to the creator, a desolate soul to my own
tender comforter. Behold, in You is everything that I
can or ought to desire. You are my salvation and
my redemption, my helper and my strength.
THOMAS Á KEMPIS

O God, whose eternal providence has embarked
our souls in the ship of our bodies, not to expect
any port of anchorage on the sea of this world,
but to steer directly through it to Your glorious
kingdom, preserve us from the dangers that on
all sides assault us, and keep our affections still
fitly disposed to receive Your holy inspirations,
that being carried strongly forward by Your
Holy Spirit we may happily arrive at
last in the haven of eternal salvation,
through our Lord Jesus Christ.
JOHN WESLEY

Seeking God

Above all things, you are to seek God. For when you do, you need look no further. For He is the answer to all questions, the light amid the darkness, the love amid the unloved, the calm within the storm, the source of all your needs. In Him, you are in want of nothing.

Every person, on coming to the knowledge of himself, is not only urged to seek God, but is also led as by the hand to find Him.
JOHN CALVIN

Lord Jesus, I am not an eagle. All I have are the eyes and the heart of one. In spite of my littleness, I dare to gaze at the sun of love, and long to fly toward it.
SAINT THÉRÈSE OF LISIEUX

O Lord my God.
Teach my heart this day
where and how to find You.
You have made me and re-made me,
and You have bestowed on me
all the good things I possess,
and still I do not know You.
I have not yet done
that for which I was made.
Teach me to seek You,
for I cannot seek You
unless You teach me,
or find You
unless You show Yourself to me.
Let me seek You in my desire;
let me desire You in my seeking.
Let me find You by loving You;
let me love You when I find You.
SAINT ANSELM

O Father, calm the turbulence of our passions;
quiet the throbbings of our hopes; repress the
waywardness of our wills; direct the motions of
our affections; and sanctify the varieties of our lot.
Be Thou all in all to us; and may all things earthly,
while we bend them to our growth in grace,
dwell lightly in our hearts, so that we may readily,
or even joyfully, give up whatever Thou dost ask
for. May we seek first Thy kingdom and
righteousness; resting assured that then all
things needful shall be added unto us.
MARY CARPENTER

Give me, O Lord, a steadfast heart, which no
unworthy affection may drag downward; give me
an unconquered heart, which no tribulation can
wear out; give me an upright heart, which no
unworthy purpose may tempt aside.
Bestow upon me also, O Lord my God,
understanding to know Thee, diligence to seek
Thee, wisdom to find Thee, and a faithfulness
that may finally embrace Thee. Amen.
SAINT THOMAS AQUINAS

O God, Thou hast found us, and not we Thee. At
times we but dimly discern Thee; the dismal mists
of earth obscure Thy glory. Yet in other and more
blessed moments, Thou dost rise upon our souls,
and we know Thee as the Light of all our seeing, the
Life of all that is not dead within us, the Bringer
of health and cure, the Revealer of peace and truth.
We will not doubt our better moments, for in them
Thou dost speak to us. We rejoice that Thou hast
created us in Thine image. Thy love has stirred us
into being, has endowed us with spiritual substance.
In the intellect, whose thoughts wander through
eternity; in the conscience that bears witness to
Thy eternal righteousness; in the affects that make
life sweet, and reach forth to Thee, O Lover of
Mankind—in these, we are made heirs
to the riches of Thy grace.
SAMUEL MCCOMB

SERVICE

When you allow yourself to be a willing servant, obeying your Master at a moment's call, you become an earthly conduit of God's heavenly blessings. But, as in all things, the first order of business is prayer, which will lead you to serve where God would have you be and to do what God would have you do.

Prayer strikes the winning blow;
service is simply picking up the pieces.
S. D. GORDON

Eternal God, who are the light of the minds that know You, the joy of the hearts that love You, and the strength of the wills that serve You; grant us so to know You, that we may truly love You, and so to love You that we may fully serve You, whom to serve is perfect freedom, in Jesus Christ our Lord.
SAINT AUGUSTINE

Lord Jesus,
I give You my hands to do Your work.
I give You my feet to go Your way.
I give you my eyes to see as You do.
I give You my tongue to speak Your words.
I give You my mind that You may think in me.
I give You my spirit that You may pray in me.
Above all, I give You my heart that you may
love in me your Father and all mankind.
I give You my whole self that You may grow
in me, so that it is You, Lord Jesus,
who live and work and pray in me.

THE GRAIL PRAYER

Speak, gracious Lord, oh speak; Thy servant hears;
For I'm Thy servant and I'll still be so;
Speak words of comfort in my willing ears;
And since my tongue is in Thy praises slow,
And since that Thine all rhetoric exceeds;
Speak Thou in words, but let me speak in deeds!

ALEXANDER POPE

I want to begin this day with thankfulness,
and continue it with eagerness. I shall be busy;
let me set about things in the spirit of service to
You and to my fellows, that Jesus knew in the
carpenter's shop in Nazareth. I am glad that He
drew no line between work sacred and secular.
Take the skill that resides in my hands, and use
it today; take the experience that life has given
me, and use it; keep my eyes open, and my
imagination alert, that I may see how things
look to others, especially the unwell, the worried,
the overlooked. For Your love's sake. Amen.

RITA SNOWDEN

Lord, send me anywhere, only go with me.
Lay any burden on me, only sustain me.
Sever any ties, but the ties that bind me
to Your heart and to Your service.

DAVID LIVINGSTONE

SIN

It's so easy to see the sins in and of others. Not so easy to see them in yourself. But God sees all. Your job? Look at yourself through God's eyes and ask for His mercy, grace, and forgiveness. Only then can you move forward and do your greatest for God.

A man by his sin may waste himself, which is to
waste that which on earth is most like God.
This is man's greatest tragedy
and God's heaviest grief.
A. W. TOZER

Lord, keep us from sinning, and make us
living witnesses of Thy mighty power
to save to the uttermost.
HANNAH WHITALL SMITH

Forgive me my sins, O Lord—the sins of my present and the sins of my past, the sins of my soul and the sins of my body, the sins which I have done to please myself and the sins which I have done to please others. Forgive me my casual sins and my deliberate sins and those which I have labored so to hide that I have hidden them even from myself. Forgive me them, O Lord, forgive them all; for Jesus Christ's sake.

THOMAS WILSON

When we think of ourselves and of the meanness and ugliness and weakness of our lives, we thank Thee for Jesus Christ our Savior. Grant unto us a true penitence for our sins. Grant that at the foot of the Cross, we may find our burdens rolled away. And so strengthen us by Thy Spirit that in the days to come, we may live more nearly as we ought. Through Jesus Christ our Lord.

WILLIAM BARCLAY

Penetrate those murky corners where we hide memories, and tendencies on which we do not care to look, but which we will not yield freely up to You, that You may purify and transmute them. The persistent buried grudge, the half-acknowledged enmity which is still smouldering; the bitterness of that loss we have not turned into sacrifice, the private comfort we cling to, the secret fear of failure which saps our initiative and is really inverted pride; the pessimism which is an insult to Your joy, Lord, we bring all these to You, and we review them with shame and penitence in Your steadfast light.

EVELYN UNDERHILL

Let us have clean hearts ready inside us for the Lord Jesus, so that He will be glad to come in, gratefully accepting the hospitality of those worlds, our hearts: He whose glory and power will endure throughout the ages. Amen.

ORIGEN

SLEEP

Thanks to your God who neither sleeps nor slumbers, you can, no matter what is happening in your life, close your eyes and lie down in peace. For when night falls, He will guard you. And when day breaks, He will sustain you.

> The bow cannot be always bent without fear of breaking. Repose is as needful to the mind as sleep to the body.
> CHARLES SPURGEON

Watch Thou, dear Lord, with those who wake, or watch, or weep tonight, and give Thine angels charge over those who sleep. Tend Thy sick ones, O Lord Christ; rest Thy weary ones; bless Thy dying ones. Soothe Thy suffering ones; shield Thy joyous ones; and all for Thy Love's sake. Amen.
SAINT AUGUSTINE

O Lord my God, I thank Thee that Thou hast brought this day to a close; I thank Thee for giving me rest in body and soul. Thy hand has been over me and has guarded and preserved me. Forgive my lack of faith and any wrong that I have done today, and help me to forgive all who have wronged us. Let me sleep in peace under Thy protection, and keep me from all the temptations of darkness. Into Thy hands I commend my loved ones and all who dwell in this house; I commend to Thee my body and soul. O God, Thy holy name be praised.

DIETRICH BONHOEFFER

O Thou, whose captain I account myself,
To Thee I do commend my watchful soul,
Ere I let fall the windows of mine eyes:
Sleeping and waking, O! defend me still.

WILLIAM SHAKESPEARE

We come before Thee, O Lord, in the end of Thy day with thanksgiving. Our beloved in the far parts of the earth, those who are now beginning the labors of the day at what time we end them, and those with whom the sun now stands at the point of noon, bless, help, console, and prosper them. Our guard is relieved, the service of the day is over, and the hour come to rest. We resign into Thy hands our sleeping bodies, our cold hearths, and open doors. Give us to awake with smiles, give us to labor smiling. As the sun returns in the east, so let our patience be renewed with dawn; as the sun lightens the world, so let our loving-kindness make bright this house of our habitation.

ROBERT LOUIS STEVENSON

The day is past and over;
All thanks, O Lord, to Thee;
I pray Thee now that sinless
The hours of dark may be:
O Jesus, keep me in Thy sight
And guard me through the night.

SAINT ANATOLIUS, translated by J. M. Neale;
"The Day Is Past and Over" hymn

Strength

In Isaiah 30:15, God says that only in submissively returning to and resting in Him will you be saved. For in the quiet of your mind and the confidence of His presence, His amazing strength will surge through you, enabling you to do what He has called and required you to do.

When a man has no strength, if he leans on God,
he becomes powerful.
D. L. Moody

O Lord our God, safe under the shadow of Your wings, let us hope. You will support us both when we are little and when we are old. When our strength is from You it is real strength, when it springs from us it is weakness. Leaning upon You we can find our way back to You, who are our refreshment and true strength. Amen.
Saint Augustine

O Thou divine Spirit, let me find my strength in
Thee. I need Thee, that I may be strong everywhere.
I long to be independent of all circumstances, alike
of the cloud and of the sunshine. I want a power to
save me from sinking in despondency, and to rescue
me from soaring in pride. I want both a pillar of
fire and a pillar of cloud; a refuge from the night of
adversity, and a shield from the day of prosperity.
I can find them in Thee. Thou hast proved Thy
power over the night and over the day. Come into
my heart, and Thy power shall be my power. I shall
be victorious over all circumstance, at home in all
scenes, restful in all fortunes. I shall have power
to tread on scorpions, and they shall do me
no hurt; the world shall be mine when
Thy Spirit is in me. Amen.
GEORGE MATHESON

God's strength flows into me continually, and is
sufficient for my every need. . . So be it; amen!
AGNES SANFORD

Lord, do not permit my trials to be above my strength; and do Thou vouchsafe to be my strength and comfort in the time of trial. Give me grace to take in good part whatever shall befall me; and let my heart acknowledge it to be the Lord's doing, and to come from Thy providence, and not by chance. . . . May I receive everything from Thy hand with patience and joy.

THOMAS WILSON

O God, who hast in mercy taught us how good it is to follow the holy desires which Thou manifoldly puttest into our hearts, and how bitter is the grief of falling short of whatever beauty our minds behold, strengthen us, we beseech Thee, to walk steadfastly throughout life in the better path which our hearts once chose; and give us the wisdom to tread it prudently in Thy fear, as well as cheerfully in Thy love; so that, having been faithful to Thee all the days of our life here, we may be able hopefully to resign ourselves into Thy hands hereafter. Amen.

Rowland Williams

STRESS

When you allow your to-dos to clutter your thinking, you squeeze God's eternal patience and presence out of your life. The key is to do what He has willed you to do and leave the rest of your duties and deadlines in His hands. In so doing, the ticking clock is silenced and you enter into God's eternal lifeline.

Eternity depends on the proper use of time.
JONATHAN EDWARDS

O gracious Father, keep me through Thy Holy Spirit; keep my heart soft and tender now in health and amidst the bustle of the world; keep the thought of Thyself present to me as my Father in Jesus Christ; and keep alive in me a spirit of love and meekness to all men, that I may be at once gentle and active and firm. O strengthen me to bear pain, or sickness, or danger, or whatever Thou shalt be pleased to lay upon me, as Christ's soldier and servant; and let my faith overcome the world daily.
THOMAS ARNOLD

Give us grace, O Lord, to work while it is day:
fulfilling diligently and patiently whatever duty
Thou appointest us, doing small things in the day
of small things, and great labors if Thou summon us
to any: rising and working, sitting still and suffering,
according to Thy word. Go with me and I will
go, but if Thou go not with me, send me not;
go before me if Thou put me forth; let me
hear Thy voice when I follow. Amen.
CHRISTINA ROSSETTI

O Lord God, in whom we live, and move, and have
our being, open our eyes that we may behold Thy
Fatherly presence ever about us. Draw our hearts to
Thee with the power of Thy love. Teach us to
be anxious for nothing, and when we have done
what Thou hast given us to do, help us, O God,
our Saviour, to leave the issue to Thy wisdom.
Take for us all doubt and mistrust. Lift our
thoughts up to Thee in heaven, and make
us to know that all things are possible to us
through Thy Son our Redeemer. Amen.
BROOKE FOSS WESTCOTT

In the name of Jesus Christ who was never in a hurry, we pray, O God, that You will slow us down, for we know that we live too fast. With all eternity before us, make us take time to live—time to get acquainted with You, time to enjoy Your blessing, and time to know each other.

PETER MARSHALL

Lord Jesus Christ, no matter where we are, far away or near at hand, off involved in the hurly-burly of life, immersed in human cares or joys, light-hearted or down in the dumps, draw us to Yourself, draw us so that we become totally Yours.

SØREN KIERKEGAARD

TEMPTATION

When you consistently and constantly abide in the anchor of Christ, the storm of temptation is of no effect. For when you are moored in God's presence, your steadfast Help and Stay proves to be more powerful and peaceful than any enticement that may flow your way.

To realize God's presence is the one sovereign remedy against temptation.
FRANCOIS FÉNELON

Blessed are all Thy saints, O God and King, who have traveled over the tempestuous sea of this life and have made the harbor of peace and felicity. Watch over us who are still on our dangerous voyage; and remember such as lie exposed to the rough storms of trouble and temptations. Frail is our vessel, and the ocean is wide; but as in Thy mercy Thou hast set our course, so steer the vessel of our life toward the everlasting shore of peace, and bring us at length to the quiet haven of our heart's desire, where Thou, O God, art blessed and livest and reignest for ever. Amen.
SAINT AUGUSTINE

Oh, teach us to know You, our God, and enable us
to do Your will as we ought to do. Give us hearts
to love You, to trust and delight in You. That no
temptations may draw us, nor any tribulations
drive us from You; but that all Your dispensations
to us, and all Your dealings with us, may be the
messengers of Your love to our souls, to bring us
still nearer to Your blessed self, and to make
us still fitter for Your heavenly kingdom.

BENJAMIN JENKS

Write Thy blessed name, O Lord, upon my heart,
there to remain so indelibly engraved, that no
prosperity, no adversity, shall ever move me from
Thy love. Be Thou to me a strong tower of defense,
a comforter in tribulation, a deliverer in distress,
a very present help in trouble, and a guide
to heaven through the many temptations
and dangers of this life.

THOMAS Á KEMPIS

Almighty God, and most merciful Father, give us, we beseech Thee, that grace that we may duly examine the inmost of our hearts, and our most secret thoughts, how we stand before Thee; and that we may henceforward never be drawn to do anything that may dishonor Thy name: but may persevere in all good purposes, and in Thy Holy service, unto our life's end; and grant that we may now this present day, seeing it is as good as nothing that we have done hitherto, perfectly begin to walk before Thee, as becometh those that are called to an inheritance of light in Christ.

GEORGE HICKES

Strong Son of God, who was tried and tempted to the uttermost, yet without sin; be near me now with Thy strength and give me the victory over this evil desire that threatens to ruin me. I am weak, O Lord, and full of doubts and fears. There are moments when I am afraid of myself, when the world and the flesh and the devil seem more powerful than the forces of good. But now I look to Thee in whom dwelleth all the fullness of grace and might and redemption. Blessed Savior! I take Thee afresh to be my Refuge, my Covert, my Defense, my strong Tower from the enemy. Hear me and bless me now and ever. Amen.

SAMUEL MCCOMB

THANKFULNESS

Because God makes all things work to your benefit, you can raise your voice in thankful song for both the evil and the good. Your part is to trust that God is doing His part—and doing it well. May He who sees the future help you to be thankful for all things present.

The unthankful heart discovers no mercies; but let the thankful heart sweep through the day and, as the magnet finds the iron, so it will find, in every hour, some heavenly blessings!

HENRY WARD BEECHER

Thou hast given so much to me
Give one thing more—a grateful heart:
Not thankful when it pleaseth me,
As if Thy blessings had spare days,
But such a heart whose pulse
may be Thy praise.

GEORGE HERBERT

Eternal and ever-blessed God, we give Thee thanks, as the day comes to an end, for those who mean so much to us, and without whom life could never be the same. We thank Thee for those to whom we can go at any time and never feel a nuisance. We thank Thee for those to whom we can go when we are tired, knowing that they have, for the weary feet, the gift of rest. We thank Thee for those with whom we can talk, and keep nothing back, knowing that they will not laugh at our dreams or mock at our failures. We thank Thee for those in whose presence it is easier to be good. We thank Thee for those in whose company joys are double dear, and sorrow's bitterness is soothed. We thank Thee for those who by their warning counsel and their rebuke have kept us from mistakes we might have made, and sins we might have committed. And above all we thank Thee for Jesus, the pattern of our lives, the Lord of our hearts, and the Savior of our souls. Accept this our thanksgiving, and grant us tonight a good night's rest; through Jesus Christ our Lord.

WILLIAM BARCLAY

O God, from whose unfailing bounty we draw our life and all that we possess, forgive our pride and self-sufficiency. Teach us to reverence the earth, which Thou hast made fruitful. Help us to remember our unity with those by whose work we are fed and clothed. Touch us with compassion for all who have not enough to eat. As Thou hast given us the knowledge which can produce plenty, so give us also the wisdom to bring it within the reach of all: through Jesus Christ our Lord.

JOHN OLDHAM

Our Father. . . We thank You for all Your mercies. Blessings have come to us in abundant measure. The evils we dreaded when the week began, have not come. The clouds we thought we saw gathering, and which we feared would bring darkness and storm —were either blown away from our sky, or coming, brought only gentle rains which have blessed our fields, leaving them more fertile. The labors we feared would be too great for our strength, have been endured, and we have had strength for them as they came. We thank You, too, for all the blessings of the week, which came to us in so many ways —through Your providences, through our friends, through our work. We have had bread to eat, and clothing to wear. We have had health and life's comforts. You have not once failed us! Amen.

J. R. MILLER

Father, with thankful and humble hearts we appear before Thee. We would thank Thee for all the benefits that we have received from Thy goodness: It is to Thy blessing we owe what success we have found. Every opportunity for doing good; every impulse in the right way; each victory we have gained over ourselves; every thought of Thy presence, O Father; every silent but loving glance on the example of our Pattern, Thy Son our Lord—all are alike. Thy gifts to us. Give us strength and wisdom to walk faithfully and joyfully in the way of willing obedience to Thy laws, and cheerful trust in Thy love. The best thanksgiving we can offer to Thee is to live according to Thy holy will; grant us every day to offer it more perfectly, and to grow in the knowledge of Thy will and the love thereof for evermore. Amen.

MICHAEL SAILER

THOUGHTS

Proverbs 23:7 says whatever you think in your heart you become. So "set your affection on things above, not on things on the earth" (Colossians 3:2), and "whatsoever things are lovely, whatsoever things are of good report; if there be any virtue, and if there be any praise, think on these things" (Philippians 4:8). What are your thoughts?

> Our life always expresses the result
> of our dominant thoughts.
> SØREN KIERKEGAARD

God is what thought cannot better; God is whom thought cannot reach; God no thinking can even conceive. Without God, men can have no being, no reason, no knowledge, no good desire, naught. Thou, O God, art what Thou art, transcending all.
ERIC MILNER-WHITE

O God,
be all my love,
all my hope,
all my striving;
let my thoughts and words flow from You,
my daily life be in You,
and every breath I take be for You.
JOHN CASSIAN

Almighty God, who alone gavest us the breath
of life, and alone canst keep alive in us the breathing
of our holy desires, we beseech Thee for Thy
compassion's sake to sanctify all our thoughts and
endeavors, that we may neither begin any action
without a pure intention, nor continue it without
Thy blessing; and grant that, having the eyes of our
understanding purged to behold things invisible
and unseen, we may in heart be inspired with
Thy wisdom, and in work be upheld by Thy
strength, and in the end be accepted of Thee,
as Thy faithful servants, having done all things
to Thy glory, and thereby to our endless
peace. Grant this prayer, O Lord. Amen.
ROWLAND WILLIAMS

O Lord of life, and Lord of love! Love us into life, and give us life to love Thee. Grant us life enough to put life into all things, that when we travel through this part of our life, and it seems but dust and barrenness, we may be full of hope in Thee. Touch this barrenness, till all things bloom. Lord, forgive us that our life is so poor, and grant us thoughts of God that we may be enabled for the time to come to make this very desert blossom. Grant that the Spirit of God may so come and so dwell, that the beauty of the Lord may be upon us: through Jesus Christ our Lord. Amen.

GEORGE DAWSON

We pray shut us out from the world's clamour and the wagging tongues and the noisy booming voices, and the example that would lead us not toward Thee, but toward the world. Save us from it and shut us in with Thee, and may we think and talk and meditate on holy things today. This message now with Thy blessing may grace and mercy and peace be with us through Jesus Christ our Lord.

A. W. TOZER

TRUST

Every heart that trusts in and is open to receive the presence of God has a special dwelling place within it, one reserved just for the Creator of the Universe. It is this kind of perfect trust and firm belief in your Father that will fill you with the strength and power to do the seemingly impossible.

When trust is perfect and there is no doubt, prayer is simply the outstretched hand ready to receive.
E. M. BOUNDS

May today there be peace within. May you trust God that you are exactly where you are meant to be. May you not forget the infinite possibilities that are born of faith. May you use those gifts that you have received, and pass on the love that has been given to you. May you be content knowing you are a child of God. Let this presence settle into your bones, and allow your soul the freedom to sing, dance, praise and love. It is there for each and every one of us.
SAINT THÉRÈSE OF LISIEUX

Infinite One who fills the universe with Your unsearchable presence, and has a dwelling-place in every heart that trusts in You: I come now in a spirit of thanksgiving, and I would commune with You in prayer that I may learn to live in Your constant presence. Indeed, may I learn to pray as I ought in spirit and in truth.

JAMES MARTINEAU

O Lord God Almighty, Who givest power to the faint, and increasest strength to them that have no might! Without Thee I can do nothing, but by Thy gracious assistance I am enabled for the performance of every duty laid upon me. Lord of power and love, I come, trusting in Thine Almighty strength, and Thine infinite goodness, to beg from Thee what is wanting in myself, even that grace which shall help me such to be, and such to do, as Thou wouldest have me. O my God! let Thy grace be sufficient for me, and ever present with me, that I may do all things as I ought. I will trust in Thee, in Whom is everlasting strength.

BENJAMIN JENKS

O Thou Eternal, in whose appointment our life standeth! Thou hast committed our work to us, and we would commit our cares to Thee. May we feel that we are not our own, and that Thou wilt heed our wants, while we are intent upon Thy will. May we never dwell carelessly or say in our hearts, "I am here, and there is none over me"; nor anxiously, as though our path were hid; but with a mind simply fixed upon our trust, and choosing nothing but the dispositions of Thy Providence.

JAMES MARTINEAU

It has pleased Thee to hide from us a perfect
knowledge, yet Thou callest for a perfect trust in
Thee. We cannot see tomorrow, we know not the
way that we take, darkness hangs about our path
and mystery meets us at every turn. Yet Thou hast
shut us up to a final faith in goodness, justice,
truth; that loving these for themselves alone,
we may find the love that passeth knowledge,
and look upon Thy face. . . . Amen.
WILLIAM EDWIN ORCHARD

Dear Jesus. . .how foolish of me to have called
for human help when You are here.
CORRIE TEN BOOM

TRUTH

Jesus is the Way, the Life, and the Truth. And the Holy Spirit is the one who, when you are homed in on Him, will guide you into all God's truth. When you obscure, mask, disguise, or hide from the truth, you become lost. But when you seek to reveal truth, you will not only find your way to life—but freedom itself.

> Where I found truth, there found I my God,
> who is the truth itself.
> SAINT AUGUSTINE

Make our hearts to burn within us, O Christ, as we walk with Thee in the way and listen to Thy words; that we may go in the strength of Thy presence and Thy truth all our journey through, and at its end behold Thee, in the glory of the Eternal Trinity, God for ever and ever.
ERIC MILNER-WHITE

Almighty God, who hast sent the Spirit of truth
unto us to guide us into all truth, so rule our lives by
Thy power, that we may be truthful in word, deed,
and thought. O keep us, most merciful Savior, with
Thy gracious protection, that no fear or hope may
ever make us false in act or speech. Cast out from us
whatsoever loveth or maketh a lie, and bring us all
to the perfect freedom of Thy truth; through
Jesus Christ Thy Son our Lord.
BROOKE FOSS WESTCOTT

O God, whose spirit searcheth all things, and whose
love beareth all things, encourage us to draw near
to Thee in sincerity and in truth. Save us from a
worship of the lips while our hearts are far away. Save
us from the useless labor of attempting to conceal
ourselves from Thee who searchest the heart.
Enable us to lay aside all those cloaks and
disguises which we wear in the light of day and
here to bare ourselves, with all our weakness,
disease and sin, naked to Thy sight.
Make us strong enough to bear the vision of the
truth, and to have done with all falsehood,
pretence, and hypocrisy, so that we may
see things as they are, and fear no more.
WILLIAM EDWIN ORCHARD

Our Lord, our Guide even unto death, grant us, we pray Thee, grace to follow Thee whithersoever Thou goest. In little daily duties to which Thou callest us, bow down our wills to simple obedience, patience under pain or provocation, strict truthfulness of word and manner, humility, kindness: in great acts of duty or perfection if Thou shouldest call us to them, uplift us to self-sacrifice, heroic courage, laying down of life for Thy Truth's sake or for a brother. Amen.

CHRISTINA ROSSETTI

You, O eternal Trinity, are a deep sea, into which the more I enter the more I find, and the more I find the more I seek. The soul cannot be satisfied in Your abyss, for she continually hungers after You, the eternal Trinity, desiring to see You with the light of Your light. As the heart desires the springs of living water, so my soul desires to leave the prison of this dark body and see You in truth. O abyss, O eternal Godhead, O sea profound, what more could You give me than Yourself? You are the fire that ever burns without being consumed; You consumed in Your heat all the soul's self-love; You are the fire which takes away cold; with Your light You illuminate me so that I may know all Your truth. Clothe me, clothe me with Yourself, eternal truth, so that I may run this mortal life with true obedience, and with the light of Your most holy faith.

CATHERINE OF SIENA

VISION

God has a vision of this world, of all His creation, of each and every person who takes a breath. Would that you would not be blind but open your eyes— as well as your heart, soul, mind, and spirit—to the vision He has for your life and the blessings with which He is surrounding you, seen and unseen.

When we are born again we all have visions, if we are spiritual at all, of what Jesus wants us to be, and the great thing is to learn not to be disobedient to the vision, not to say that it cannot be attained. . . . When God gives a vision, transact business on that line, no matter what the cost.
OSWALD CHAMBERS

Grant me, O Lord, the single eye, that I may see the one thing needful, the thing that You want done. Don't let my vision be blurred by looking at too many things, or longing to please anyone but You. Give me simplicity of heart, quiet confidence in You, and eagerness to know and do Your will.
GEORGE APPLETON

O Thou, who art the ever-blessed God, the underlying Peace of the world, and who wouldst draw all men into the companionship of Thy joy; speak, we beseech Thee, to this Thy servant, for whom we pray. Take him by the hand and say unto him, "Fear not; for I am with thee. I have called thee by my name; thou art mine." Put such a spirit of trust within him that all fear and foreboding shall be cast out, and that right reason and calm assurance may rule his thoughts and impulses. Let quietness and confidence be his strength. Reveal to him the vision of a universe guided and governed by Thy wise and loving care; and show him that around and about him are Thy unseen and beneficent powers.

SAMUEL MCCOMB

O God, light of the minds that see You, life of the souls that love You, and strength of the souls that seek You, enlarge our minds and raise the vision of our hearts, that, with swift wings of thought, our spirits may reach You, the eternal wisdom, You who live from everlasting to everlasting; through Jesus Christ our Lord. Amen.

SAINT AUGUSTINE

Lord, open our eyes that we may see, for the world all around us, as well as around the prophet, is full of [Your] horses and chariots, waiting to carry us to places of glorious victory. And when our eyes are thus opened, we shall see in all the events of life, whether great or small, whether joyful or sad, a "chariot" for our souls.

HANNAH WHITALL SMITH
adapted from *The Christian's Secret of a Happy Life*

Fulfill us, Lord Jesus, with the grace of Thy Holy Spirit, that everything we see may represent to us the presence, the excellency, and the power of God, and our conversation with the creatures lead us unto the Creator; that so our actions may be done more frequently with an eye to God's presence, by our often seeing him in the glass of creation; who with Thee and the Holy Spirit liveth and reigneth, ever one God, world without end. Amen.

JEREMY TAYLOR

WISDOM

Thank God for the spirit of wisdom that lightens your path. Because with God's wisdom, there is no need to ever feel lost. For every moment He gives you enough information and understanding to deepen your faith, enlarge your trust, and find your way—if only you'd ask.

There is but One, He that sitteth in heaven,
who is able to teach man wisdom.
JOHN WESLEY

Here I have seen things rare and profitable;
Things pleasant, dreadful, things to make me stable
In what I have begun to take in hand;
Then let me think on them, and understand
Wherefore they showed me were, and let me be
Thankful, O good Interpreter, to Thee.
JOHN BUNYAN

Suffer me never to think that I have knowledge
enough to need no teaching, wisdom enough to
need no correction, talents enough to need no grace,
goodness enough to need no progress, humility
enough to need no repentance, devotion enough to
need no quickening, strength enough without Thy
Spirit; lest, standing still, I fall back for evermore.
ERIC MILNER-WHITE

Strengthen me, O God, by the grace of Thy Holy
Spirit; grant me to be strengthened with might in
the inner man, and to empty my heart of all useless
care and anguish. O Lord, grant me heavenly
wisdom, that I may learn above all things to seek
and to find Thee, above all things to relish and
to love Thee, and to think of all other things
as being, what indeed they are, at the
disposal of Thy wisdom. Amen.
THOMAS Á KEMPIS

Grant unto us, Almighty God, that when our vision fails, and our understanding is darkened; when the ways of life seem hard, and the brightness of life is gone—to us grant the wisdom that deepens faith when the sight is dim, and enlarges trust when the understanding is not clear. And whensoever Thy ways in nature or in the soul are hard to be understood, then may our quiet confidence, our patient trust, our loving faith in Thee, be great, and as children knowing that they are loved, cared for, guarded, kept, may we with a quiet mind at all times put our trust in the unseen God.

GEORGE DAWSON

O God, by whom the meek are guided in judgment, and light riseth up in darkness for the godly; grant us, in all our doubts and uncertainties, the grace to ask what Thou wouldst have us to do; that the spirit of wisdom may save us from all false choices, and that in Thy light we may see light, and in Thy straight path may not stumble, through Jesus Christ our Lord.

WILLIAM BRIGHT

WORRY

There is no problem so big, no trouble so tall, no fear so terrifying, no threat so imminent that God cannot handle and subdue it. When you come to Him with worries large and small, He gently holds you, reassures you, and then exchanges them for that peace that surpasses all understanding.

Worry does not empty tomorrow of its sorrows;
it empties today of its strength.
CORRIE TEN BOOM

O most loving Father, You who will us to give thanks for all things, to dread nothing but the loss of Yourself, and to cast all our care on You, who care for us; preserve us from faithless fears and worldly anxieties, and grant that no clouds of this mortal life may hide from us the light of that love which is immortal, and which You have manifested unto us in Your Son, Jesus Christ our Lord.
WILLIAM BRIGHT

God of our secret life, weary of ourselves, we come to Your shelter. Our span of troubled days we bring within Your calm eternity. Over our path of pilgrimage, we feel the spaces of Your immensity. In the strife of life and the sadness of mortality, we find a spirit of power and of hope in Your providence. Infinite Ruler of creation, whose spirit dwells in every world: we look not to the heavens for You, though You are there; we search not in the oceans for Your presence, though it murmurs with Your voice; we wait not for the wings of the wind to bring You near, though they are Your messengers; for You are in our hearts, O God. You make Your abode in the deep places of our thought and love. In each gentle affection, each contrite sorrow, each noble aspiration, we would worship You.

JAMES MARTINEAU

O Lord, this is all my desire—to walk along the path of life that Thou hast appointed me, even as Jesus my Lord would walk along it, in steadfastness of faith, in meekness of spirit, in lowliness of heart, in gentleness of love. And because outward events have so much power in scattering my thoughts and disturbing the inward peace in which alone the voice of Thy Spirit is heard, do Thou, gracious Lord, calm and settle my soul by that subduing power which alone can bring all thoughts and desires of the heart into captivity to Thyself. All I have is Thine; do Thou with all as seems best to Thy divine will; for I know not what is best. Let not the cares or duties of this life press on me too heavily; but lighten my burden, that I may follow Thy way in quietness, filled with thankfulness for Thy mercy, and rendering acceptable service unto Thee. Amen.

MARIA HARE

Oh, Lord, unto whom all hearts are open, Thou
canst govern the vessel of my soul far better than
I can. Arise, O Lord, and command the stormy
wind and the troubled sea of my heart to be still,
and at peace in Thee, that I may look up to Thee
undisturbed, and abide in union with Thee, my
Lord. Let me not be carried hither and thither by
wandering thoughts; but forgetting all else, let me
see and hear Thee. Renew my spirit; kindle me in
Thy light, that it may shine within me, and my heart
may burn in love and adoration toward Thee. Let
Thy Holy Spirit dwell in me continually, and make
me Thy temple and sanctuary, and fill me
with divine love and light and life, with devout
and heavenly thoughts, with comfort and
strength, with joy and peace. Amen.

JOHANN ARNDT

O God, we thank Thee for this universe, our great home; for its vastness and its riches, and for the manifoldness of the life which teems upon it and of which we are a part. We praise Thee for the arching sky and the blessed winds, for the driving clouds and the constellations on high. We praise Thee for the salt sea and the running water, for the everlasting hills, for the trees, and for the grass under our feet. We thank Thee for our senses by which we can see the splendor of the morning, and hear the jubilant songs of love, and smell the breath of the springtime. Grant us, we pray Thee, a heart wide open to all this joy and beauty, and save our souls from being so steeped in care or so darkened by passion that we pass heedless and unseeing when even the thornbush by the wayside is aflame with the glory of God.

WALTER RAUSCHENBUSCH